LEVEL 6 Supplemental
ANSWER BOOK

By Glory St. Germain ARCT RMT MYCC UMTC &
Shelagh McKibbon-U'Ren RMT UMTC

The LEVEL 6 Supplemental Workbook is designed to be completed with the Intermediate Rudiments Workbook.

GSG MUSIC
Enriching Lives Through Music Education

ISBN: 978-1-927641-57-6

# The Ultimate Music Theory™ Program

The Ultimate Music Theory™ Program lays the foundation of music theory education.

The focus of the Ultimate Music Theory Program is to simplify complex concepts and show the relativity of these concepts with practical application. This program is designed to help teachers and students discover the excitement and benefits of a sound music theory education.

The Ultimate Music Theory Program is based on a proven approach to the study of music theory that follows the *"must have"* Learning Principles to develop effective learning for all learning styles.

The Ultimate Music Theory™ Program and Supplemental Workbooks help students prepare for nationally recognized theory examinations including the Royal Conservatory of Music.

GSG MUSIC

Library and Archives Canada Cataloguing in Publication
UMT Supplemental Series / Glory St. Germain and Shelagh McKibbon-U'Ren

Gloryland Publishing - UMT Supplemental Workbook and Answer Book Series:

GP-SPL	ISBN: 978-1-927641-41-5	UMT Supplemental Prep Level
GP-SL1	ISBN: 978-1-927641-42-2	UMT Supplemental Level 1
GP-SL2	ISBN: 978-1-927641-43-9	UMT Supplemental Level 2
GP-SL3	ISBN: 978-1-927641-44-6	UMT Supplemental Level 3
GP-SL4	ISBN: 978-1-927641-45-3	UMT Supplemental Level 4
GP-SL5	ISBN: 978-1-927641-46-0	UMT Supplemental Level 5
GP-SL6	ISBN: 978-1-927641-47-7	UMT Supplemental Level 6
GP-SL7	ISBN: 978-1-927641-48-4	UMT Supplemental Level 7
GP-SL8	ISBN: 978-1-927641-49-1	UMT Supplemental Level 8
GP-SCL	ISBN: 978-1-927641-50-7	UMT Supplemental Complete Level
GP-SPLA	ISBN: 978-1-927641-51-4	UMT Supplemental Prep Level Answer Book
GP-SL1A	ISBN: 978-1-927641-52-1	UMT Supplemental Level 1 Answer Book
GP-SL2A	ISBN: 978-1-927641-53-8	UMT Supplemental Level 2 Answer Book
GP-SL3A	ISBN: 978-1-927641-54-5	UMT Supplemental Level 3 Answer Book
GP-SL4A	ISBN: 978-1-927641-55-2	UMT Supplemental Level 4 Answer Book
GP-SL5A	ISBN: 978-1-927641-56-9	UMT Supplemental Level 5 Answer Book
GP-SL6A	ISBN: 978-1-927641-57-6	UMT Supplemental Level 6 Answer Book
GP-SL7A	ISBN: 978-1-927641-58-3	UMT Supplemental Level 7 Answer Book
GP-SL8A	ISBN: 978-1-927641-59-0	UMT Supplemental Level 8 Answer Book
GP-SCLA	ISBN: 978-1-927641-60-6	UMT Supplemental Complete Level Answer Book

Respect Copyright - Copyright 2017 Gloryland Publishing

All rights reserved. No part of this publication may be reproduced or transmitted in any form or by any means, electronic or mechanical, including photocopying, recording, or any information storage and retrieval system, without permission in writing from the author/publisher.

* Resources - An annotated list is available at UltimateMusicTheory.com under Free Resources.

Ultimate Music Theory

LEVEL 6 Supplemental

Table of Contents

Ultimate Music Theory	The Story of UMT… Meet So-La & Ti-Do	4
Comparison Chart	Level 6	6
Note and Rest Values	Rhythm Review and Beaming Notes	8
Enharmonic Equivalent	Whole Steps (Chromatic and Diatonic)	14
Key Relationship	Relatives, Parallel, Enharmonic Scales	16
Scale Degrees	Writing Scales with Key Signatures & Accidentals	18
Rhythm and Beams	Grouping Notes in Simple and Compound Time	20
Beams and Rests	Time Signatures - Simple Time and Compound Time	22
Chromatic Alteration	Enharmonic Equivalent Intervals	24
Chord Symbols	Major and minor, Dominant Seventh	27
Open/Close Position	Major/minor triads, Dominant Seventh chords, SATB Texture	28
Open/Close Position	Dominant Seventh Chords and Triads	32
Harmonic Analysis	Broken Triads/Chords (Major, minor, Dominant Seventh	35
Excerpt Analysis	Musical Excerpt Analysis Steps - Grand Staff	36
Alberti Bass	Writing Broken Chord Patterns	37
Italian Terms	Combining Italian Terms and Definitions	38
Lead Sheets	Rewriting a Melody with Lead Sheets	39
Cadences	Authentic and Half Cadences Identification	40
Transposition	Major and minor keys - Modulation in Music	42
Motive and Sequence	Monophonic, Homophonic and Polyphonic Texture	44
Melody Writing	Parallel Period and Analysis and Harmonic Progression	46
Binary Form	Simple, Balanced, Barform, Rounded Binary & Ternary	52
Melody Writing	Imagine, Compose, Explore & Sight Reading - The Lizard	56
Music History	Baroque Era (1600 - 1750) - Early, Middle and Late	58
J. S. Bach	Invention in C Major No. 1 BWV 772	60
J. S. Bach	Analysis of Brandenburg Concerto No. 5 First Movement	64
W. A. Mozart	Analysis of Eine kleine Nachtmusik First Movement	68
Tempo Term Review	Game - Ti-Do's Tempo Trail	72
Theory Exam	Level 6	73
Certificate	Completion of Level 6	80

Score: **60 - 69** Pass; **70 - 79** Honors; **80 - 89** First Class Honors; **90 - 100** First Class Honors with Distinction

Ultimate Music Theory: *The Way to Score Success!*

Workbooks, Exams, Answers, Online Courses, App & More!

A Proven Step-by-Step System to Learn Theory Faster - from Beginner to Advanced.

Innovative techniques designed to develop a complete understanding of music theory, to enhance sight reading, ear training, creativity, composition and musical expression.

All UMT Series have matching Answer Books!

The UMT Rudiments Series - Beginner A, Beginner B, Beginner C, Prep 1, Prep 2, Basic, Intermediate, Advanced & Complete (All-In-One)

- ♪ 12 Lessons, Review Tests, and a Final Exam to develop confidence
- ♪ Music Theory Guide & Chart for fast and easy reference of theory concepts
- ♪ 80 Flashcards for fun drills to dramatically increase retention & comprehension

Rudiments Exam Series - Preparatory, Basic, Intermediate & Advanced

- ♪ 8 Exams plus UMT Tips on How to Score 100% on Theory Exams

Each Rudiments Workbook correlates to a Supplemental Workbook.

The UMT Supplemental Series - Prep Level, Level 1, Level 2, Level 3, Level 4, Level 5, Level 6, Level 7, Level 8 & Complete (All-In-One) Level

- ♪ Form & Analysis and Music History - Composers, Eras & Musical Styles
- ♪ Melody Writing using ICE - Imagine, Compose & Explore
- ♪ 12 Lessons, Review Tests, Final Exam and 80 Flashcards for quick study

Supplemental Exam Series - Level 5, Level 6, Level 7 & Level 8

- ♪ 8 Exams to successfully prepare for nationally recognized Theory Exams

UMT Online Courses, Music Theory App & More

- ♪ UMT Certification Course, Teachers Membership & Elite Educator Program
- ♪ Ultimate Music Theory App correlates to the Rudiments Workbooks
- ♪ Free Resources - Teachers Guide, Music Theory Blogs, videos & downloads

Go To: **UltimateMusicTheory.com**

At Ultimate Music Theory we are passionate about helping teachers and students experience the joy of teaching and learning music by creating the most effective music theory materials on the planet!

Introducing the Ultimate Music Theory Family!

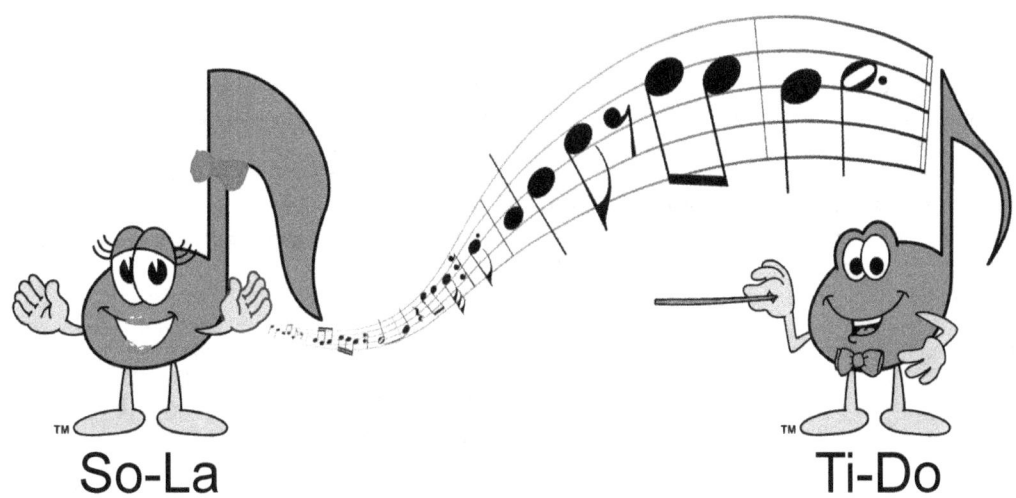

So-La

Meet So-La! So-La loves to sing and dance.

She is expressive, creative and loves to tell stories through music!

So-La feels music in her heart. She loves to teach, compose and perform.

Ti-Do

Meet Ti-Do! Ti-Do loves to count and march.

He is rhythmic, consistent and loves the rules of music theory!

Ti-Do feels music in his hands and feet. He loves to analyze, share tips and conduct.

So-La & Ti-Do will guide you through Mastering Music Theory!

Enriching Lives Through Music Education

The Ultimate Music Theory™ Comparison Chart to the 2016 Royal Conservatory of Music Theory Syllabus.
Level 6

The Ultimate Music Theory™ Rudiments Workbooks, Supplemental Workbooks and Exams prepare students for successful completion of the Royal Conservatory of Music Theory Levels.

UMT Intermediate Rudiments Workbook plus the LEVEL 6 Supplemental Workbook = RCM Theory Level 6.
♫ Note: Additional completion of the LEVEL 7 Supplemental Workbook = RCM Theory Level 7.

RCM Level 6 Theory Concept	Ultimate Music Theory Intermediate Workbook
Required Keys - Major and minor keys up to seven sharps and flats	**Keys Covered** - Major and minor keys up to seven sharps and flats * Workbook Pages - Identifying the Key of a Melody
Pitch and Notation - Accidentals: double sharp and double flat - Transposition of melodies in Major keys up by any interval within an octave	**Pitch and Notation Covered** - Accidentals: double sharp and double flat - Transposition of melodies in Major keys up by any interval within an octave * Workbook Pages - Whole Step and Enharmonic Equivalent Review
Scales and Scale Degree Names - Major and minor scales (natural, harmonic and melodic forms) up to seven sharps or flats (using key signatures and/or accidentals) - Relative Major/minor keys, enharmonic equivalents - Parallel Major/minor keys, enharmonic equivalents - Scale Degrees (Tonic, Supertonic, Mediant, Subdominant, Dominant, Submediant, Leading Tone and Subtonic)	**Scales and Scale Degree Names Covered** - Major and minor scales (natural, harmonic and melodic forms) up to seven sharps or flats (using key signatures and/or accidentals) * Workbook Page - Scale Review using Scale Degree Names - Relative Major and minor keys, including enharmonic equivalents - Parallel (or "Tonic") Major and minor keys and Scales, including enharmonic equivalents * Workbook Pages - Parallel Scales Review - Scale Degrees (Tonic, Supertonic, Mediant, Subdominant, Dominant, Submediant, Leading Note and Subtonic) * Workbook Page - Leading Tone (Leading Note) or Subtonic Review * Workbook Page - Scales and Scale Degree Notes Review - Chromatic Scales (Harmonic and Melodic) - 20th Century Scales - Whole Tone, Pentatonic, Blues and Octatonic
Rhythm and Meter - Note and Rest Values: breve, whole, half, quarter, eighth, sixteenth and thirty-second notes and rests (including dotted sixteenth notes and rests) - New Compound Time: 6/4, 9/4, 12/4, 6/8, 9/8, 12/8, 6/16, 9/16, 12/16 - Application of Time Signatures, bar lines, notes and rests	**Rhythm and Meter Covered** - Note and Rest Values: breve, whole, half, quarter, eighth, sixteenth and thirty-second notes and rests * Workbook Pages - Rhythm Review - Writing Notes and Rests; Beams and Dotted Notes; Adding Bar Lines in Simple & Compound Time - Time Signatures: Simple Time and Compound Time - Application of Time Signatures, bar lines, notes and rests * Workbook Pages - Rewriting Rhythms, Adding Bar Lines and Rests
Intervals - All Intervals (Major, minor, Perfect, Augmented, diminished) within an octave above a given note (using Key Signatures or Accidentals) - Enharmonic Equivalent Intervals	**Intervals Covered** - All Intervals (Major, minor, Perfect, Augmented, diminished) within an octave above a given note (using Key Signatures or Accidentals) - Inversions of Intervals * Workbook Pages - Enharmonic Equivalent Intervals (Chromatically Altering Upper or Lower Notes)
Musical Terms and Signs - Tempo, Dynamics and Articulation	**Musical Terms and Signs Covered** * Workbook Pages - Musical Terms and Signs * Workbook Page Bonus - Analysis and Sight Reading

RCM Level 6 Theory Concept (Continued)

Chords and Harmony

- Solid/Blocked or Broken Triads of Major and minor quality, root position and inversions, in Major and harmonic minor scales, close or open position

- Dominant 7th Chords, Root Position, in close or open position

- Application of Functional or Root/Quality Chord Symbols for the implied harmonies of a melody, using root position I, i, IV, iv or V chords
- Identification of Authentic (V - I or V - i) and half cadences (I - V; IV - V or i - V; iv - V) on a Grand Staff, using root position triads in Major and minor keys, in keyboard style

Form and Analysis

- Identification of concepts from this and previous levels within short music examples
- Identification of the key (Major or minor) of a given passage with or without a Key Signature

Melody and Composition

- Composition of a question-answer phrase pair (antecedent-consequent) in a Major key, given the first two measures to create a Parallel Period

Music History/Appreciation

Guided Listening: "Invention in C Major, BWV 772" by Johann Sebastian Bach. Listening Focus: Invention, Concerto Grosso, Polyphonic Texture, Motive, Sequence

Guided Listening: "Brandenburg Concerto No. 5", First Movement, by Johann Sebastian Bach. Listening Focus: Invention, Concerto Grosso, Polyphonic Texture, Motive, Sequence

Guided Listening: "Eine kleine Nachtmusik", First Movement by Wolfgang Amadeus Mozart. Listening Focus: Chamber Music, Homophonic Texture, Sonata Form (Exposition, Development and Recapitulation)

Examination

Level 6 Theory Examination

Ultimate Music Theory Intermediate Workbook (Continued)

Chords and Harmony Covered

- Solid/Blocked or Broken Triads of Major and minor quality, root position and inversions, in Major and harmonic minor scales, close or open position
* Workbook Pages - Root/Quality Chord Symbols - Triads on Scale Degrees of Major and harmonic minor scales
* Workbook Pages - Dominant 7th Chord, Root Position, in close or open position (including Root/Quality and Functional Chord Symbols)
* Workbook Pages - Rewriting Close Position Triads into Open Position
* Workbook Pages - Application and Analysis of Root/Quality and Functional Chord Symbols for the implied harmonies of a melody, using root position (I, i, IV, iv, V, V^7) Chords
- Cadences - Perfect (Authentic), Plagal and Imperfect (Half) on a Grand Staff, in Keyboard Style, in Major and minor keys using root position triads
* Workbook Pages - Cadence Identification Review

Form and Analysis Covered

* Workbook Pages - Identification of concepts from this and previous levels within short music examples
- Identification of the key (Major or minor) of a given passage with or without a Key Signature

Melody and Composition Covered

* Workbook Pages - Composition of a question-answer phrase pair (antecedent-consequent) in a Major key, given the first two measures to create a Parallel Period

Music History/Appreciation Covered

* Workbook Pages - "Invention in C Major, BWV 772" by Johann Sebastian Bach. Listening Focus: Invention, Concerto Grosso, Polyphonic Texture, Motive, Sequence
Free Resources for Listening Activities & Watching Videos
* Workbook Pages - "Brandenburg Concerto No. 5", First Movement, by Johann Sebastian Bach. Listening Focus: Invention, Concerto Grosso, Polyphonic Texture, Motive, Sequence
Free Resources for Listening Activities & Watching Videos
* Workbook Pages - "Eine kleine Nachtmusik", First Movement by Wolfgang Amadeus Mozart. Listening Focus: Chamber Music, Homophonic Texture, Sonata Form (Exposition, Development and Recapitulation)
Free Resources for Listening Activities & Watching Videos

Review Tests & Final Exam

- 12 Accumulative Review Tests (1 with each of the 12 Lessons)
* UMT Level 6 Theory Exam
* UMT Exam Series - Intermediate Rudiments

Get your **UltimateMusicTheoryApp.com** - Over 7000 Flashcards including audio! Learn Faster with all 6 Subjects: Beginner - Prep, Basic, Intermediate, Advanced, Ear Training & Music Trivia (including History).

Intermediate Music Theory App Subject - Use with the Intermediate Workbook 12 Decks - 1,312 Cards

1 - Notation, Key Signature & Simple Time
3 - Double Sharps & Flats and Scales
5 - 5 - Simple Time and Compound Time
7 - Triads & Inversions, Close & Open Position
9 - Rewrite a Melody using a Key Signature
11 - Transposition - Major Key to Major Key

2 - Circle of Fifths, Major and Enharmonic Scales
4 - Technical Degrees & Chromatic Scales
6 - Intervals (Aug & dim) and Inversions
8 - Whole Tone, Pentatonic, Octatonic Scales
10 - Cadences - Perfect, Plagal and Imperfect
12 - Analysis, Italian Terms and Signs

NOTES AROUND the WORLD - Use after Intermediate Page 9

Notes - The signs representing the length of sound (notes) have different names in different languages.

So-La Says: No matter what the language, each note still receives the same value of sound.

Note Sign	English (American)	English (British)	French	Italian
𝄺	Double-whole note	Breve (or Brevis)	Double-ronde (or brevis)	Breve
o	Whole note	Semibreve	Ronde (or semi-breve)	Semibreve
𝅗𝅥	Half note	Minim	Blanche	Minima (or bianca)
♩	Quarter note	Crotchet	Noire	Semiminima (or nera)
♪	Eighth note	Quaver	Croche	Croma
𝅘𝅥𝅯	Sixteenth note	Semiquaver	Double croche	Semicroma
𝅘𝅥𝅰	Thirty-second note	Demisemiquaver	Triple croche	Biscroma

The bottom number of Time Signature = Type of Note that receives one Basic Beat.

♪ **Ti-Do Tip:** "British" English is the English language as used in the United Kingdom.

1. Scoop each Basic Beat. Write the Basic Beat (Half note, Minim, Blanche) below each scoop. Add bar lines to complete the following measures.

2. Circle the correct answer for each of the following:

   a) In 3/2 Time, a half note receives: **(1 Basic Beat)** or 2 Basic Beats or 4 Basic Beats.

   b) In "British" English, a half note is called a: Breve or Semibreve or **(Minim.)**

   c) In French, a half note is called a: Double-ronde or **(Blanche)** or Ronde.

RESTS AROUND the WORLD - Use after Intermediate Page 9

Rests - The signs representing the length of silence (rests) have different names in different languages.

Note Sign	English (American)	English (British)	French	Italian
𝄺	Double-whole rest	Breve rest	Pause de breve	Pausa di breve
𝄻	Whole rest	Semibreve rest	Pause	Pausa di semibreve
𝄼	Half rest	Minim rest	Demi-pause	Pausa di minima
𝄽	Quarter rest	Crotchet rest	Soupir	Pausa di seminima
𝄾	Eighth rest	Quaver rest	Demi-soupir	Pausa di croma
𝄿	Sixteenth rest	Semiquaver rest	Quart de soupir	Pausa di semicroma
𝅀	Thirty-second rest	Demisemiquaver rest	Huiti-me de soupir	Pausa di biscroma

So-La Says: No matter what the language, each rest still receives the same value of silence.

Rests are drawn in the same position on the Treble and Bass Staff.

♩ **Ti-Do Tip:** A whole rest is used for a whole measure of silence in any Time Signature except $\frac{4}{2}$.

1. Write the Basic Beat and Pulse below each measure. Add rests below each bracket (Crotchet rest or Soupir, Quaver rest or Demi-soupir, Semiquaver rest or Quart de soupir) to complete each measure.

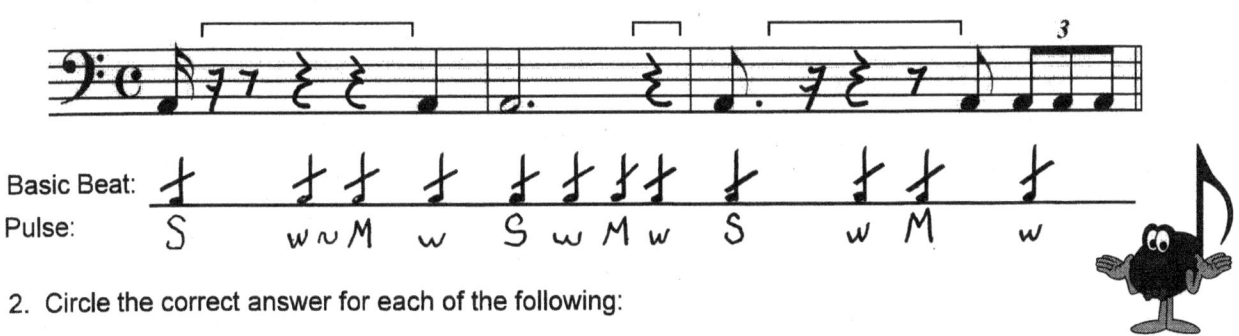

2. Circle the correct answer for each of the following:

   a) In 𝄴 Time, a quarter rest receives: (**1 Basic Beat**) or 2 Basic Beats or 4 Basic Beats.

   b) In "British" English, a quarter rest is called a: Semibreve rest or Minim rest or (**Crotchet rest**).

   c) In French, a quarter rest is called a: (**Soupir**) or Demi-soupir or Pause.

RHYTHM REVIEW - MUSIC, MATH and DOTTED NOTES - Use after Intermediate Page 9

Dotted Notes - A dot adds half the value of the note.

> **So-La Says:** Math and Music work together to establish the value of the dot for each note.
>
> Each note can be divided in half: The value of the dot = half the value of the note:
>
> Breve note: 𝄺 = o + o   Dotted Breve note: 𝄺• = 𝄺 + o
>
> Whole note: o = ♩ + ♩   Dotted Whole note: o• = o + ♩
>
> Half note: ♩ = ♩ + ♩   Dotted Half note: ♩• = ♩ + ♩
>
> Quarter note: ♩ = ♪ + ♪   Dotted Quarter note: ♩• = ♩ + ♪
>
> Eighth note: ♪ = ♬ + ♬   Dotted Eighth note: ♪• = ♪ + ♬
>
> Sixteenth note: ♬ = 𝅘𝅥𝅱 + 𝅘𝅥𝅱   Dotted Sixteenth note: ♬• = ♬ + 𝅘𝅥𝅱

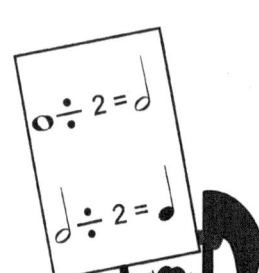

$o \div 2 = \text{♩}$

$\text{♩} \div 2 = \text{♩}$

♫ **Ti-Do Tip:** Mathematical Equations show how Music and Math are connected. Have fun!

1. Use Math and Music to solve the following! Write one note (or one dotted note) that equals the value of the notes when added together.

   a) ♩ + ♩ + ♩ = __o•__   b) ♪ + ♪ + ♪ = __♩•__

   c) ♬ + ♬ + ♬ = __♪•__   d) ♩ + ♩ + ♩ = __♩•__

   e) o + o + o = __𝄺•__   f) o + ♩ + ♩ = __𝄺__

   g) ♬ + ♬ + ♬ = __♪__   h) ♪ + ♪ + ♪ = __♩__

   i) ♬ + ♬ + ♬ + ♬ = __♪__   j) ♪ + ♪ + ♪ + ♪ = __♩__

   k) ♬ + ♬ + ♬ + ♬ = __♪•__   l) ♪ + ♪ + ♪ + ♪ = __♩•__

RHYTHM REVIEW - MUSIC = MATH - Use after Intermediate Page 9

In "American" English, the **Names of Notes** have their foundation in mathematical fractions.

So-La Says: The names of the notes are the same as the names of fractions in math!

MUSIC = MATH!

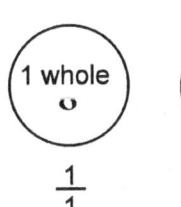 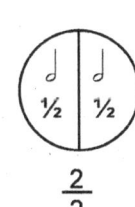 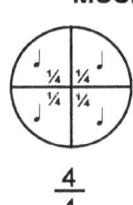  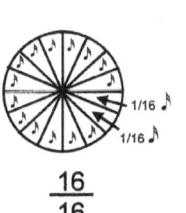 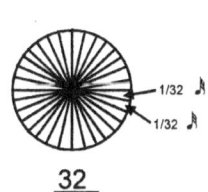

$$\frac{1}{1} \qquad \frac{2}{2} \qquad \frac{4}{4} \qquad \frac{8}{8} \qquad \frac{16}{16} \qquad \frac{32}{32}$$

NOTES = FRACTIONS!

The name of each note is a fraction that can be divided into groups of "2".

1 whole = 2 halves = 4 quarters = 8 eighths = 16 sixteenths = 32 thirty-seconds

1 x 𝅝 = 2 x 𝅗𝅥 = 4 x ♩ = 8 x ♪ = 16 x ♬ = 32 x 𝅘𝅥𝅰

A **"dot"** changes the fractions into groups of "3".

1 dotted whole = 3 halves = 6 quarters = 12 eighths = 24 sixteenths = 48 thirty-seconds

1 x 𝅝· = 3 x 𝅗𝅥 = 6 x ♩ = 12 x ♪ = 24 x ♬ = 48 x 𝅘𝅥𝅰

♫ **Ti-Do Tip:** A Fraction has a line called a "Vinculum" (or fraction bar) between the upper and lower numbers. A Time Signature does **not** have a line between the upper and lower numbers.

1. Following the examples, use Note Names and Numbers to show the following Math = Music Equations.

   a) 1 whole note = 2 __half__ notes = 4 __quarter__ notes; 1 x 𝅝 = 2 x 𝅗𝅥 = 4 x ♩.

   b) 1 dotted whole note = 3 __half__ notes = 6 __quarter__ notes; 1 x 𝅝· = 3 x 𝅗𝅥 = 6 x ♩.

   c) 1 eighth note = 2 __sixteenth__ notes = 4 __thirty-second__ notes; 1 x ♪ = 2 x ♬ = 4 x 𝅘𝅥𝅰.

   d) 1 dotted eighth note = 3 __sixteenth__ notes = 6 __thirty-second__ notes; 1 x ♪· = 3 x ♬ = 6 x 𝅘𝅥𝅰.

   e) 1 quarter note = 2 __eighth__ notes = 4 __sixteenth__ notes; 1 x ♩ = 2 x ♪ = 4 x ♬.

   f) 1 dotted quarter note = 3 __eighth__ notes = 6 __sixteenth__ notes; 1 x ♩· = 3 x ♪ = 6 x ♬.

   g) 1 half note = 2 __quarter__ notes = 4 __eighth__ notes; 1 x 𝅗𝅥 = 2 x ♩ = 4 x ♪.

   h) 1 dotted half note = 3 __quarter__ notes = 6 __eighth__ notes; 1 x 𝅗𝅥· = 3 x ♩ = 6 x ♪.

RHYTHM REVIEW - BEAMING NOTES - Use after Intermediate Page 9

Beaming Notes - Beams (horizontal lines) are used to join notes together.

A single beam is used to group eighth notes (♪ ♪), a double beam is used to group sixteenth notes (♬) and a triple beam is used to group thirty-second notes (♬).

> **So-La Says:** A Dotted Eighth note is often joined with a Sixteenth note; a Dotted Sixteenth note is often joined with a Thirty-Second note.
>
> When "flagged" notes are joined together, beams (horizontal lines) are used instead of the flags.
>
>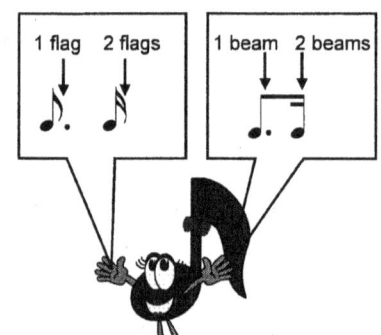
>
> Dotted Eighth note + Sixteenth note = ♪. + ♪ = ♪.♪
>
> Dotted Sixteenth note + Thirty-Second note = ♬. + ♬ = ♬.♬
>
> Sixteenth note + Dotted Eighth note = ♪ + ♪. = ♪♪.
>
> Thirty-Second note + Dotted Sixteenth note = ♬ + ♬. = ♬♬.

♫ **Ti-Do Tip:** It is preferable to use a beam (or beams) to group the notes according to each Basic Beat.

 Beams are written at the end of the stems, grouping notes together. For thirty-second notes, extend the length of the stem one extra space to have room to write 3 beams.

1. Following the example, rewrite each group of notes using beams to form one quarter note Basic Beat.

2. Rewrite the following rhythm, beaming the notes to show the quarter note Basic Beats.

Basic Beat:

RHYTHM REVIEW - BASIC BEATS and BEAMS - Use after Intermediate Page 9

Basic Beat - The top number of the Time Signature indicates the number of Basic Beats per measure. The bottom number of the Time Signature indicates the kind of note that equals one Basic Beat.

Eighth notes, Sixteenth notes and Thirty-Second notes are beamed together according to the Basic Beat.

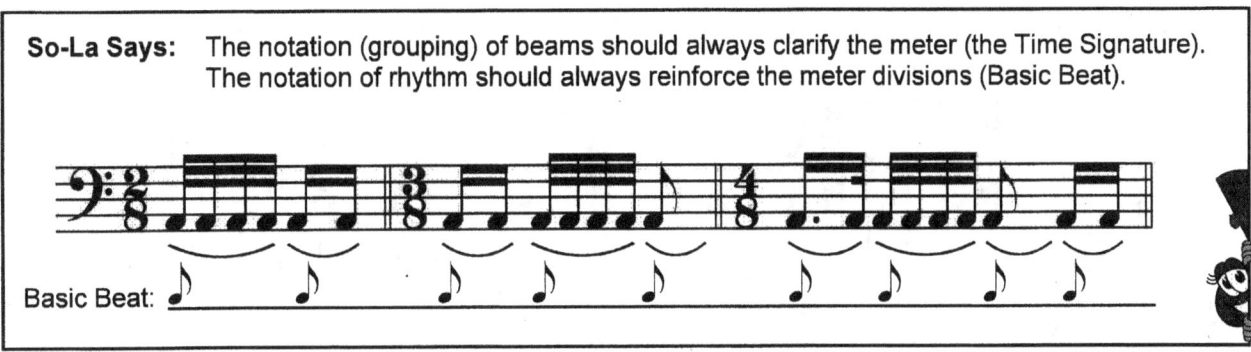

♫ **Ti-Do Tip:** Each Basic Beat is indicated by a scoop (a visual representation of one Basic Beat).

1. Following the example, add stems and beams to create groups of notes that equal one quarter note Basic Beat.

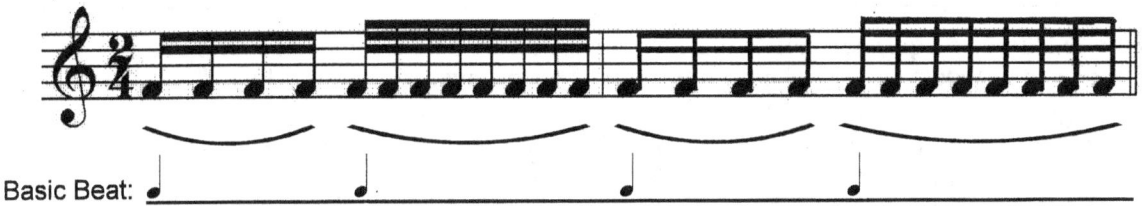

2. Following the example, add stems and beams to create groups of notes that equal one eighth note Basic Beat.

3. Following the example, add stems and beams to create groups of notes that equal one sixteenth note Basic Beat.

ENHARMONIC EQUIVALENT REVIEW - Use after Intermediate Page 32

Accidentals are signs that raise or lower the pitch of a note.

By using double sharps, sharps, (naturals), flats and double flats, each key on the keyboard can be written using 2 or 3 different letter names. These are called **Enharmonic Equivalent** Notes.

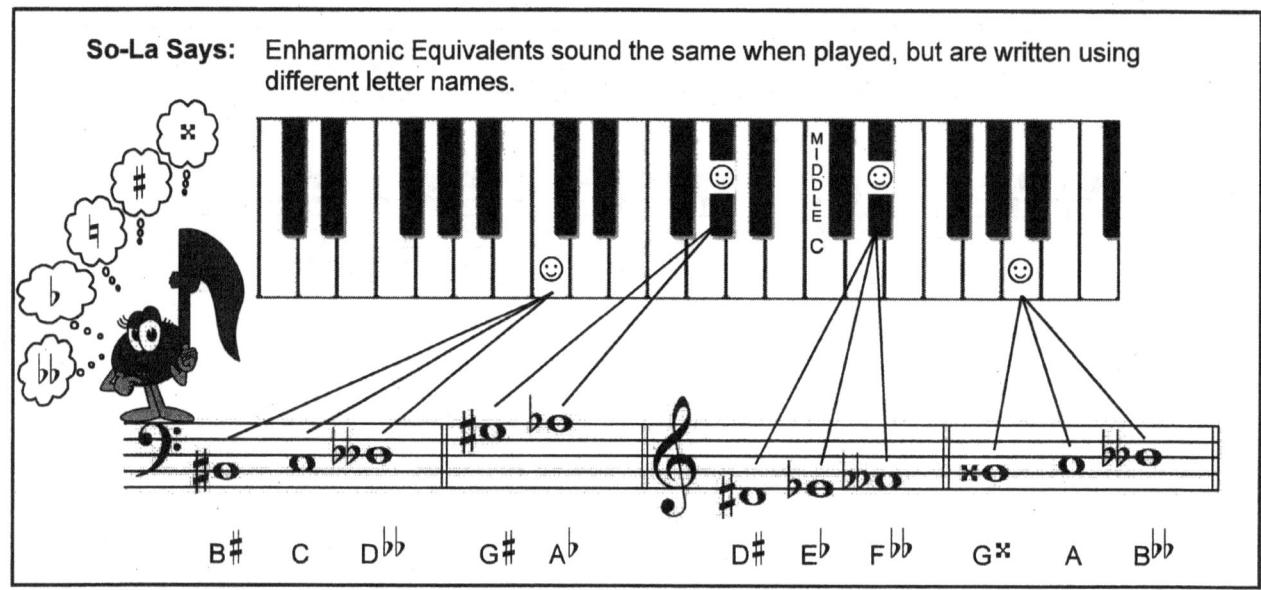

1. Write all the Enharmonic Equivalent note names for each key on the keyboard indicated with a ☺. Observe the pitch of Middle C. Use whole notes and any necessary accidentals. Name the notes.

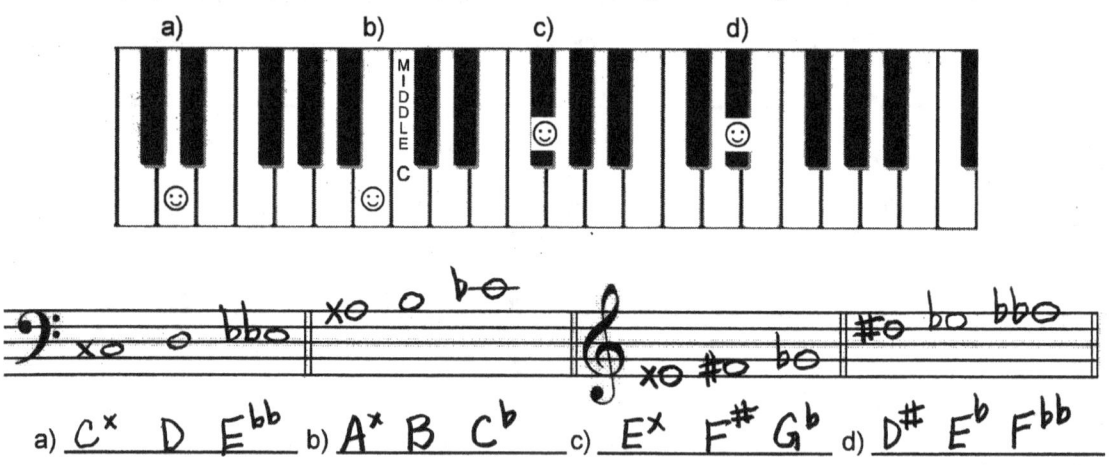

2. Write two notes that are the Enharmonic Equivalents for each given note. Use whole notes and any necessary accidentals.

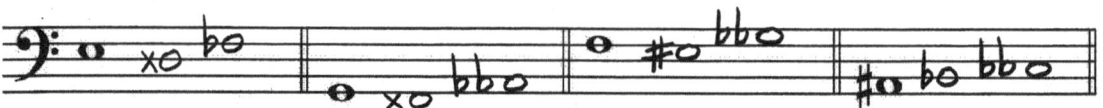

> ♪ **Ti-Do Time:** Play the Enharmonic Equivalent Notes on your instrument at the correct pitch. Listen - are the notes at the same pitch?

WHOLE STEP REVIEW - Use after Intermediate Page 32

A **Whole Step** is the distance from one key to another with one key in between. A Whole Step is also called a Whole Tone or Tone. A Whole Step equals two half steps (semitones).

Chromatic Whole Step - an interval of a 1st written using the same letter names (B - B𝄪).

Diatonic Whole Step - an interval of a 2nd written using neighboring (next door) letter names (B - C♯).

Not a Whole Step - an interval of a 3rd written skipping a letter name (B - D♭). An interval distance of a whole step written as an interval of a 3rd is called a "diminished third" (a half step smaller than a minor third).

> **So-La Says:** A whole step written in different ways still remains at the same pitch (sound).

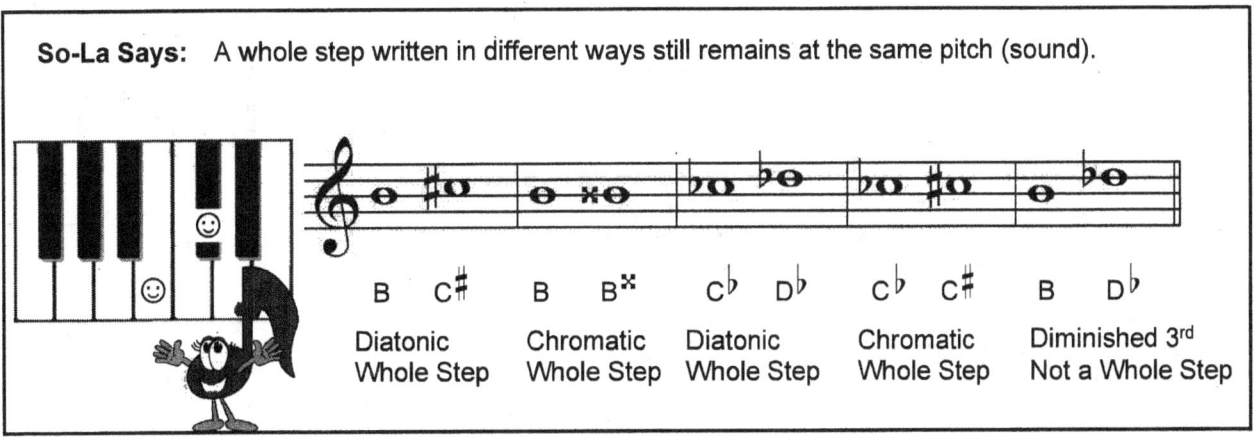

> ♩ **Ti-Do Tip:** Unless it is specifically requested to write a Chromatic Whole Step, the distance of a "Whole Step" refers to a Diatonic Whole Step (interval of a 2nd, using neighboring letter names).

1. Write the second note in each measure a Whole Step (or Chromatic Whole Step as indicated) above the given notes. Use whole notes. Name the notes.

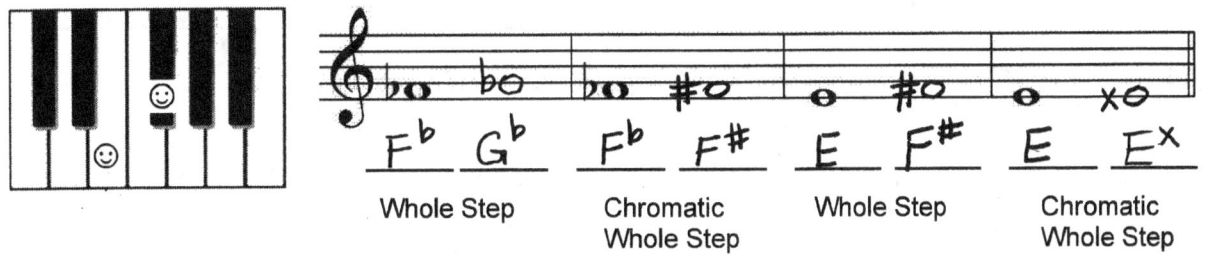

2. Create a Whole Step by adding an accidental to the second note in each measure. Name the notes.

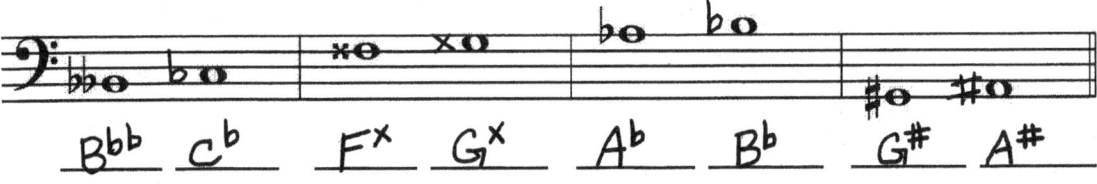

> ♩ **Ti-Do Time:** Play these distances on your instrument. Can you hear the difference between a (Diatonic) Whole Step and a Chromatic Whole Step?

KEY RELATIONSHIP REVIEW - Use after Intermediate Page 41

There are many ways for different Keys to have a relationship. They can be connected through the same Key Signature, the same Tonic note or the same pitch (Enharmonic Equivalents).

Relative Major and minor keys - Same Key Signature, different Tonic Notes.
   Example: The Relative minor key of D Major is b minor; the Relative Major key of b minor is D Major.

Parallel (or Tonic) Major and minor keys - Same Tonic Note, different Key Signatures.
   Example: The Parallel (Tonic) minor key of D Major is d minor; the Parallel Major of d minor is D Major.

Enharmonic Parallel (or Tonic) Major and/or minor keys - Same Pitch, different letter names.
   Example: The Enharmonic Parallel (Tonic) minor of D♭ Major is c♯ minor;
   The Enharmonic Parallel (Tonic) Major of c♯ minor is D♭ Major;
   The Enharmonic Parallel (Tonic) Major of C♯ Major is D♭ Major;
   The Enharmonic Parallel (Tonic) minor of b♭ minor is a♯ minor.

Enharmonic Relative Major and/or minor keys - Begin on the same pitch as the relative Major or minor, but use different letter names.
   Example: The Enharmonic Relative minor of G♭ Major is d♯ minor;
   The Enharmonic Relative Major of a♭ minor is B Major.

 **So-La Says:** Discovering the relationships between Keys is like being a Detective!

To discover the Enharmonic Relative Major and/or minor key:

Step #1: Identify the Relative Major or minor key.

Step #2: Identify the Enharmonic name for that key.

Question: Name the Enharmonic Relative Major key of e♭ minor.
   Step #1: Relative Major key of e♭ minor: G♭ Major
   Step #2: Enharmonic name of G♭: F♯
   Answer: The Enharmonic Relative Major key of e♭ minor is F♯ Major.

♫ **Ti-Do Tip:** To discover the Enharmonic Parallel (or Tonic) Major or minor key, identify the Enharmonic name of the Tonic note.

1. Name each of the following keys and the Key Signature of the new key.

a) The Relative minor key of F♯ Major is __d♯ minor__ Key Signature: __F♯ C♯ G♯ D♯ A♯ E♯__.

b) The Tonic minor key of B♭ Major is __b♭ minor__ Key Signature: __B♭ E♭ A♭ D♭ G♭__.

c) The Tonic Major key of b minor is __B Major__ Key Signature: __F♯ C♯ G♯ D♯ A♯__.

d) The Enharmonic Parallel (Tonic) minor key of d♯ minor is __e♭ minor__ Key Signature: __B♭ E♭ A♭ D♭ G♭ C♭__.

e) The Enharmonic Parallel (Tonic) Major key of B Major is __C♭ Major__ Key Signature: __B♭ E♭ A♭ D♭ G♭ C♭ F♭__.

f) The Enharmonic Relative minor key of D♭ Major is __a♯ minor__ Key Signature: __F♯ C♯ G♯ D♯ A♯ E♯ B♯__.

g) The Enharmonic Relative Major key of g♯ minor is __C♭ Major__ Key Signature: __B♭ E♭ A♭ D♭ G♭ C♭ F♭__.

SCALE REVIEW - Use after Intermediate Page 41

Review Lessons 1 - 3 of the **Ultimate Music Theory Intermediate Workbook**: Scale patterns of Whole Tones (Whole Steps) and Half Steps (Semitones) of Major and minor (natural, harmonic and melodic), relative Major/minor, Tonic Major/minor scales and more.

 **So-La Says:** When asked to write a **Relative** Major or minor scale, a **Parallel** (Tonic) Major or minor scale, an **Enharmonic Tonic** scale or an **Enharmonic Relative** scale:

Step #1: Identify the name of the scale based on the question. (To support the identification of Key Relationships, write the Circle of Fifths on your Whiteboard.)

Step #2: Write the scale. Follow the instructions to use accidentals or to use a Key Signature (and any necessary accidentals for a harmonic or melodic scale).

1. Identify the name of the scale based on the question. Write the scale as directed (using a Key Signature or accidentals), ascending and descending. Use whole notes.

   a) The Enharmonic Tonic minor scale, melodic form, of E♭ Major, using accidentals.
   Name of scale: __d♯ minor melodic__

   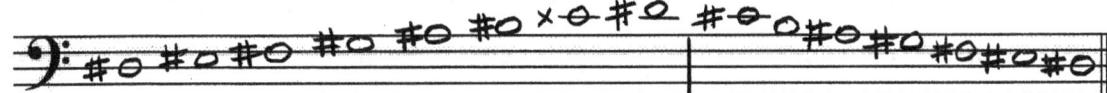

   b) The natural minor scale that is the Parallel (Tonic) minor of F Major, using accidentals.
   Name of scale: __f minor natural__

   c) The Tonic Major scale of b minor, using a Key Signature.
   Name of scale: __B Major__

   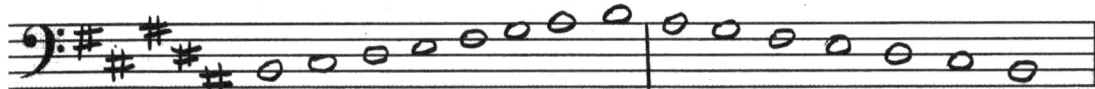

   d) The Enharmonic Relative minor scale, harmonic form, of G♭ Major, using a Key Signature.
   Name of scale: __d♯ minor harmonic__

   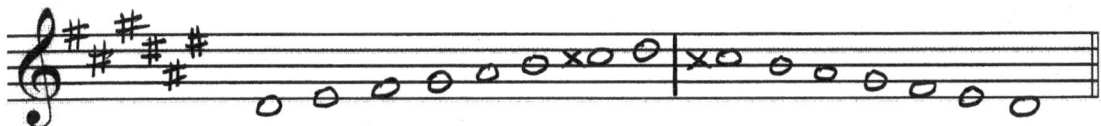

♪ **Ti-Do Time:** Your Teacher will play the scales on Page 17. Identify the scale as a Major, natural minor, harmonic minor or melodic minor scale.

SCALE DEGREE REVIEW - LEADING TONE or SUBTONIC - Use after Page 46

Review Page 24 of the **Ultimate Music Theory LEVEL 5 Supplemental Workbook**: Scale Degree Numbers and Technical Degree Names.

Scale Degree Numbers are numbers with a circumflex, caret sign or hat (^) written above the number.

Technical Degree Names are names used to identify the degrees of a scale.

> **So-La Says:** The **Leading Tone** (Leading Note) is always a half step (semitone) below the Tonic.
> The **Subtonic** is always a whole step (whole tone) below the Tonic.
>
> In melodic minor scales, degrees $\hat{6}$ and $\hat{7}$ are different in the ascending and descending scales.
> **Ascending melodic minor scale**: Degree $\hat{7}$ is a half step below the Tonic = **Leading Tone**.
> **Descending melodic minor scale**: Degree $\hat{7}$ is a whole step below the Tonic = **Subtonic**.
>
> In Major, natural minor and harmonic minor scales, the ascending and descending notes are the same.
> **Major scale**: Degree $\hat{7}$ is a half step below the Tonic = **Leading Tone**.
> **Harmonic minor scale**: Degree $\hat{7}$ is a half step below the Tonic = **Leading Tone**.
> **Natural minor scale**: Degree $\hat{7}$ is a whole step below the Tonic = **Subtonic**.

♩ **Ti-Do Tip:** When using a Key Signature, an accidental will be needed to write the Leading Tone of a minor key. An accidental will not be needed to write the Subtonic of a minor key.

1. a) Write the Key Signature on the Grand Staff.
   b) Write the note in both the Treble and Bass Staves. Use whole notes and accidentals if needed.

a) Leading Tone of e♭ minor   b) Subtonic of b minor   c) Supertonic of C♯ Major   d) Leading Tone of D♭ Major

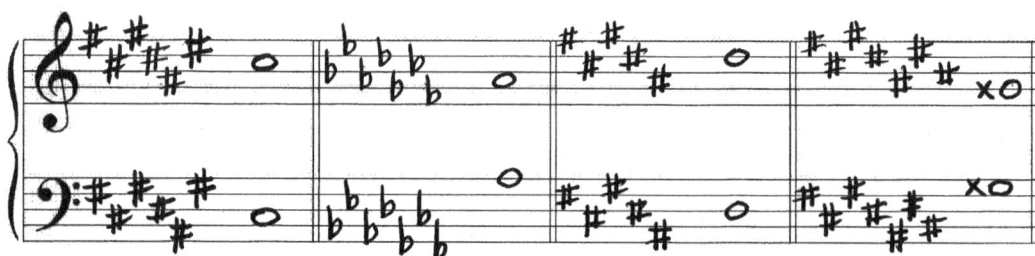

e) Subtonic of d♯ minor   f) Submediant of C♭ Major   g) Mediant of B Major   h) Leading Tone of a♯ minor

SCALE REVIEW - WRITING SCALES BASED ON A TECHNICAL DEGREE NAME - Use after Page 46

Be a Detective and use the Scale Degree Name of a note to identify which Scale to write!

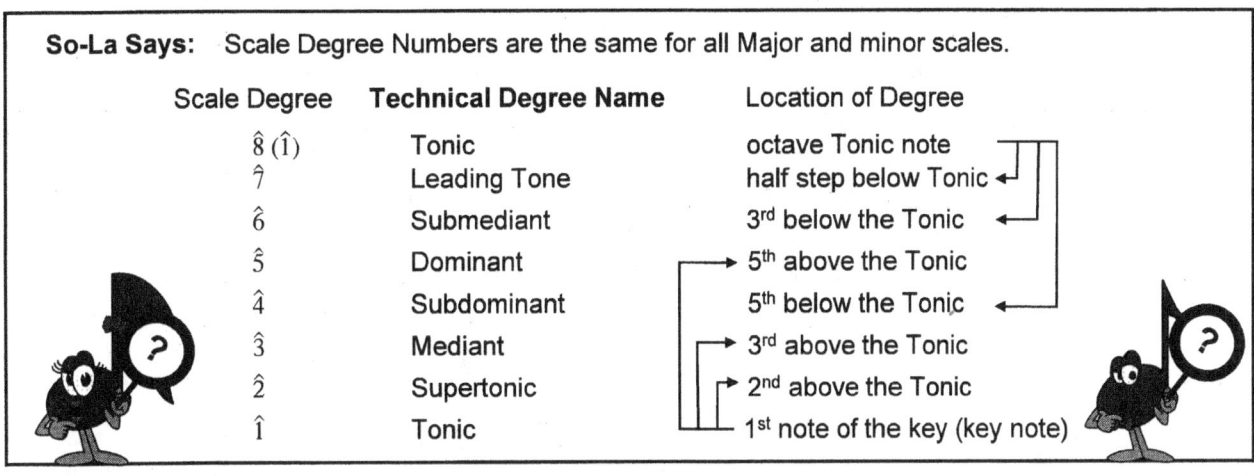

So-La Says: Scale Degree Numbers are the same for all Major and minor scales.

Scale Degree	Technical Degree Name	Location of Degree
$\hat{8}$ ($\hat{1}$)	Tonic	octave Tonic note
$\hat{7}$	Leading Tone	half step below Tonic
$\hat{6}$	Submediant	3rd below the Tonic
$\hat{5}$	Dominant	5th above the Tonic
$\hat{4}$	Subdominant	5th below the Tonic
$\hat{3}$	Mediant	3rd above the Tonic
$\hat{2}$	Supertonic	2nd above the Tonic
$\hat{1}$	Tonic	1st note of the key (key note)

♪ **Ti-Do Tip:** A note that is a Whole Step below the Tonic is called the Subtonic (Sub = below).

1. Identify the name of the scale based on the question. Write the scale as directed (using a Key Signature or accidentals), ascending and descending. Use whole notes.

a) The harmonic minor scale with D as the Supertonic ($\hat{2}$), using a Key Signature.
   Name of scale: _C minor harmonic_

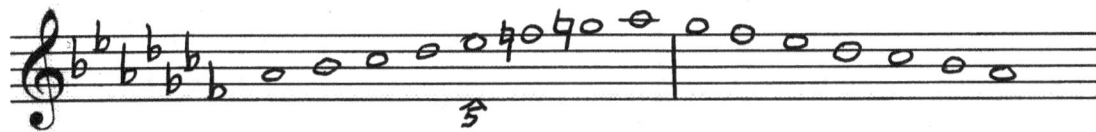

b) The melodic minor scale with E♭ as the Dominant ($\hat{5}$), using a Key Signature.
   Name of scale: _a♭ minor melodic_

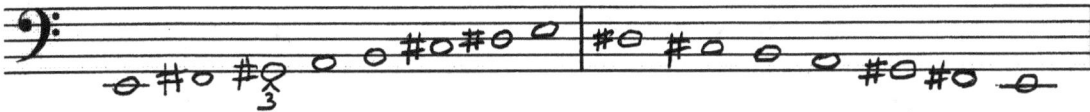

c) The Major scale with G♯ as the Mediant ($\hat{3}$), using accidentals.
   Name of scale: _E Major_

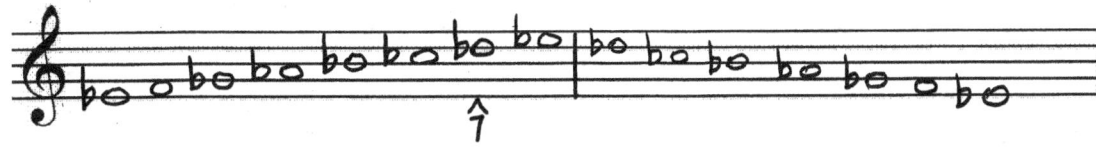

d) The natural minor scale with D♭ as the Subtonic ($\hat{7}$), using accidentals.
   Name of scale: _e♭ minor natural_

RHYTHM REVIEW - REWRITING RHYTHMS using CORRECT BEAMS - Use after Page 61

The word "**Rhythm**" comes from the Greek word "**Rhythmos**" which means "any regular recurring motion or symmetry". In Music, notes are clearly grouped to establish a Simple Time Rhythm or a Compound Time Rhythm.

Review Page 14 of the **Ultimate Music Theory LEVEL 5 Supplemental Workbook**: Introduction to Compound Time.

Memorize the **Strong (S), weak (w)** and **Medium (M) Pulses** in Simple Time and the **Strong dot (S·), weak dot (w·)** and **Medium dot (M·) Pulses** in Compound Time.

So-La Says: In Simple Time, beamed notes are grouped together for each Basic Beat. In Compound Time, they are grouped together for each Compound Basic Beat.

1. a) Rewrite each pattern of "No Rhythm" Notes into a Simple Time Rhythm and into a Compound Time Rhythm. Group (beam) the notes together to correctly show the Basic Beat and Pulse.
   b) Scoop the equal groups. Write the Basic Beat (or Compound BB) and Pulse below each rhythm.

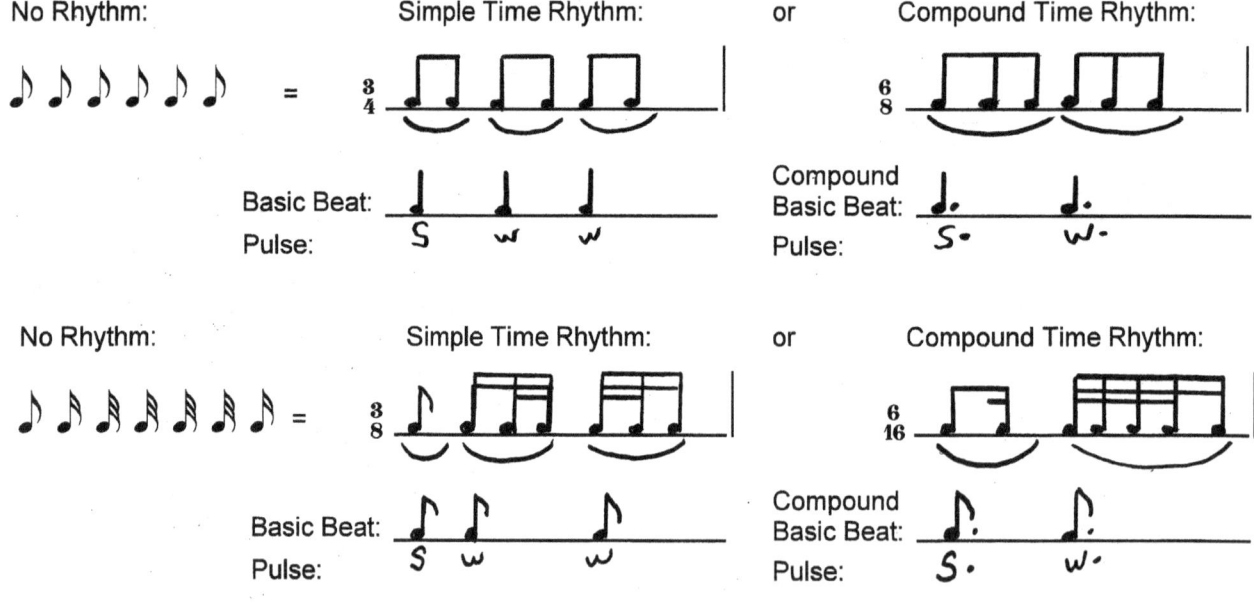

♪ **Ti-Do Time:** Pulse is the "Heart Beat" of the Rhythm. Play the "**Rhythm-Pulse Game**". First clap the "no rhythm" notes - do not pulse. (Isn't it boring?) Then clap either the Simple Time Rhythm or the Compound Time Rhythm (with pulse). Ask your Teacher to tell you which Rhythm you clapped!

RHYTHM REVIEW - ADDING TIME SIGNATURES - Use after Intermediate Page 61

The **rhythm** of the notes, how the notes are grouped (especially the beaming of the Eighth, Sixteenth and Thirty-Second notes), will establish whether the **Time Signature** is Simple or Compound.

> **So-La Says:** To add a Time Signature, look for the clues in the rhythm that establish a **Simple Rhythm** or a **Compound Rhythm**.
>
> Clue: Dotted Rests are not used in Simple Time; Dotted Rests are used in Compound Time.
>
> Clue: Beams in Simple Time are in groups of "2"; Beams in Compound Time are in groups of "3".

♪ **Ti-Do Tip:** To check your work, it is okay to write in the Scoops, Basic Beats/Compound Basic Beats and/or Pulses (even when the instructions do not ask you to do this).

1. Add the correct Time Signature below each bracket.

a)

b)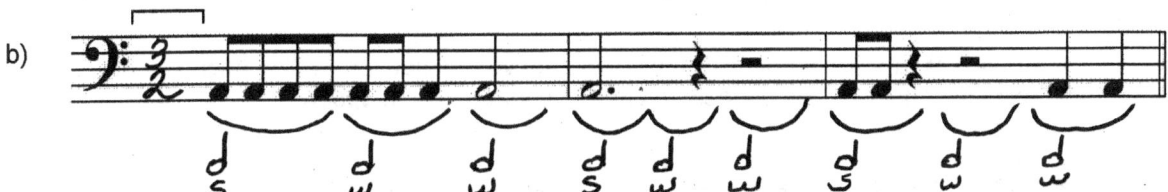

c)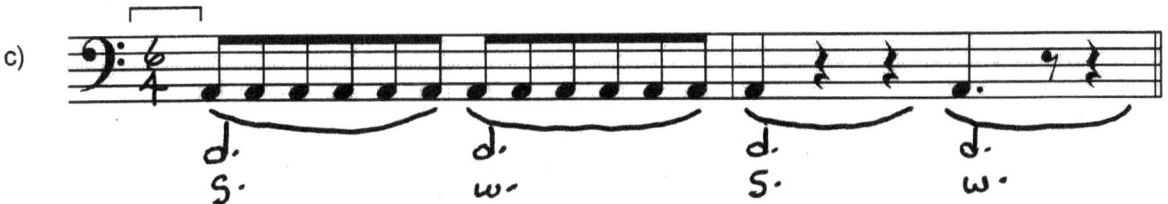

d)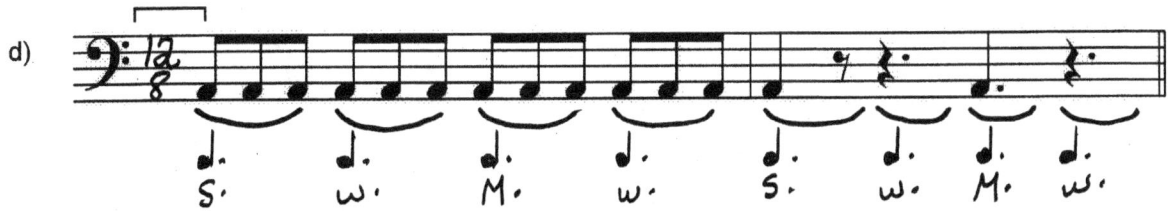

> ♪ **Ti-Do Time:** Rhythms can use the same type of notes and lengths of silence, but have different Time Signatures based upon the grouping of the notes and rests.
>
> Clap rhythms a & b, and rhythms c & d. Clap the pulses clearly. What is the same and what is different?

UltimateMusicTheory.com © Copyright 2017 Gloryland Publishing. All Rights Reserved.

BEAMS and RESTS REVIEW - Use after Intermediate Page 65

Notes and rests are grouped according to each **Basic Beat** and each **part of a Basic Beat**.

When adding missing rests, beams will be used to establish what type of rests need to be used and which Basic Beat (or part of a Basic Beat) to which the rest belongs.

Separated Beams (a separation in the beam/beams; when eighth, sixteenth and thirty-second notes are not joined together) indicate that the notes do not belong to the same Basic Beat.

Joined Beams (no separation in the beams) indicate that the notes belong to the same Basic Beat. This will affect how rests are added (and what types of rests will be required to complete the measure).

> **So-La Says:** Separated Beams = different Basic Beat, not part of the same Basic Beat.
> Joined Beams = part of the same Basic Beat.
>
> Step #1: Using scoops, establish which notes will be in the same or in different Basic Beats.
>
> Step #2: Add Basic Beats (and any necessary scoops) to complete the Measure. Add the rests.
>
>
>
> The spacing in the measure, and the length of the brackets above the measure, will support proper placement of any extra scoops/Basic Beats/rests needed to complete the measure.

♪ **Ti-Do Tip:** Placing too many Basic Beats below a shorter bracket creates a "squished" appearance.

1. a) Using scoops, establish which notes will be in the same or in different Basic Beats.
   b) Add Basic Beats (and any necessary scoops) to complete the Measure. Add the rests.

WHOLE REST REVIEW - Use after Intermediate Page 65

A **Whole Rest** is used for a whole measure of silence in all Simple & Compound Time Signatures except $\frac{4}{2}$.

In $\frac{4}{2}$, a **Breve Rest** (or **Double Whole Rest**) is used for a whole measure of silence (S + w + M + w). A Whole Rest is used to group Basic Beats 1 & 2 (S + w) and Basic Beats 3 & 4 (M + w) into one rest.

In $\frac{3}{2}$, a **Whole Rest** is used for a whole measure of silence (S + w + w). A Whole Rest is also used to group Basic Beats 1 & 2 (S + w) into one rest.

> **So-La Says:** **Plus (+) sign:** For the Basic Beat Pulse, join the S + w (+ w) or the M + w (+ w).
> For the Compound Basic Beat Pulse, join the S· + w· or the M· + w·.
>
> **Tilde (~) sign:** For the Basic Beat Pulse, do not join the w ~ M or the w ~ w.
> For the Compound Basic Beat Pulse, do not join the w· ~ M· or the w· ~ w·.

♪ **Ti-Do Tip:** **Show your work!** Use Scoops, Basic Beats, Pulses, Plus & Tilde signs to find the answers.

1. The rests in each measure on the top (first) staff are incorrect. Following the example, on the staff below the incorrect staff, rewrite the rhythm and use the correct rests. (Show your work!)

a) Incorrect:

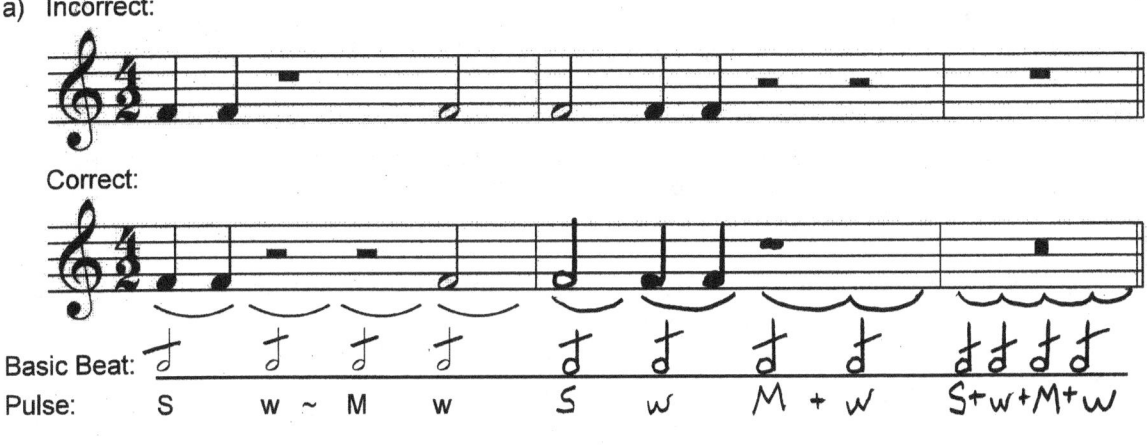

b) Incorrect:

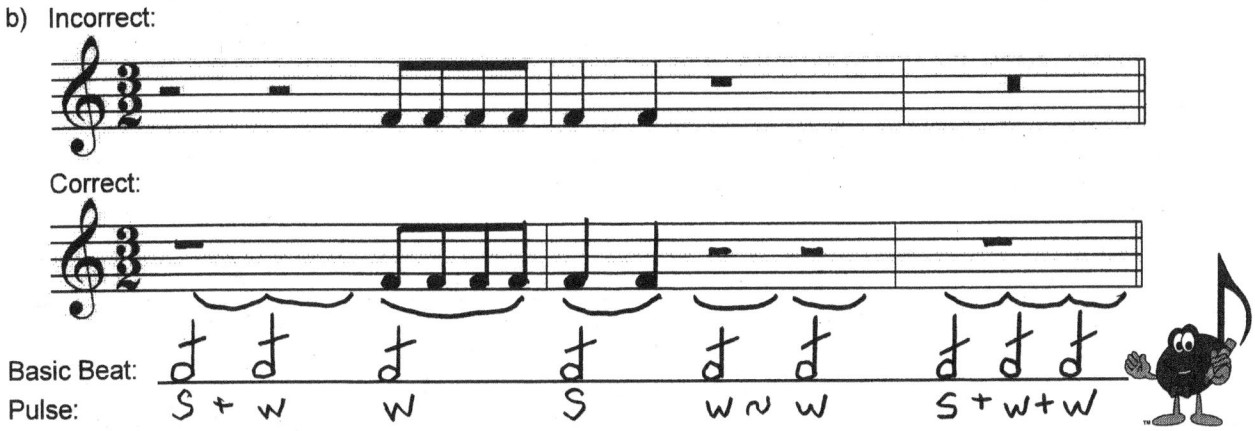

CHROMATIC ALTERATION - LARGER - Use after Intermediate Page 78

An Interval is the distance in pitch between two notes. An interval is defined by a **Number** and a **Quality**.

Review Pages 26, 27, 28 and 29 of the **Ultimate Music Theory LEVEL 5 Supplemental Workbook**: Intervals.

Intervals can be written and identified using accidentals and using a Key Signature. Intervals can be written and identified in music in Homophonic Texture, Monophonic Texture and/or Polyphonic Texture (using Single Stemming or Double Stemming).

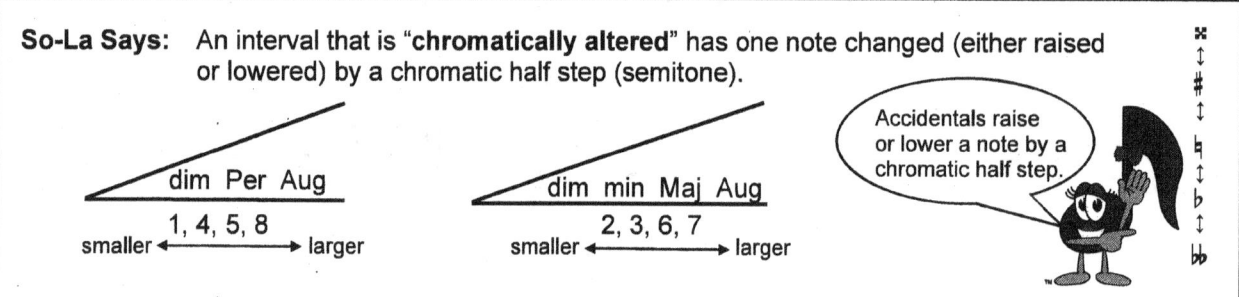

♪ Ti-Do Tip: Chromatic Alteration → Original Interval → New Interval Quality

Half step (semitone) **larger**:
- raise the upper (top) note;
- lower the bottom note.

Original	becomes	New
minor		Major
Major		Augmented
diminished		minor or Perfect
Perfect		Augmented

When writing intervals using accidentals (with or without bar lines), **accidentals** may be required to raise or lower the chromatically altered note. Observe any bar lines when rewriting or altering intervals.

1. a) Name the given interval.
   b) Rewrite the interval, Chromatically Altering the interval to make it larger by raising the upper (top) note by a chromatic half step. Name the new interval.

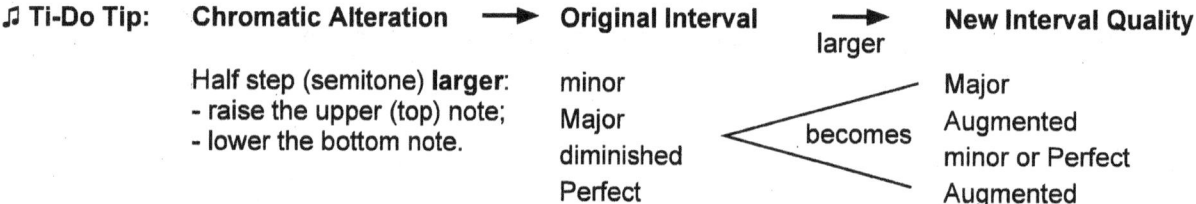

min 6   Maj 6   Per 4   Aug 4   Maj 3   Aug 3

2. a) Name the given interval.
   b) Rewrite the interval, Chromatically Altering the interval to make it larger by lowering the bottom note by a chromatic half step. Name the new interval.

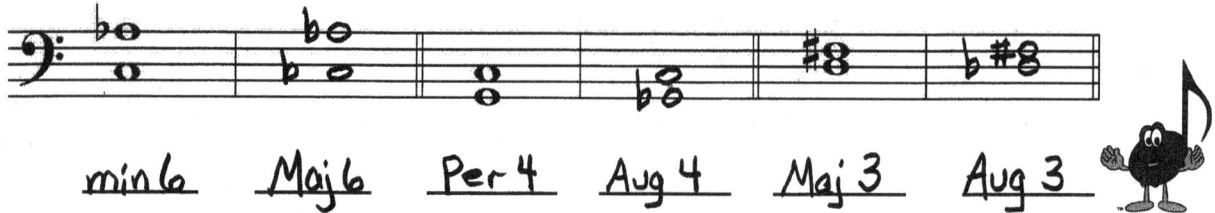

min 6   Maj 6   Per 4   Aug 4   Maj 3   Aug 3

UltimateMusicTheory.com © Copyright 2017 Gloryland Publishing. All Rights Reserved.

CHROMATIC ALTERATION - SMALLER - Use after Intermediate Page 78

When Chromatically Altering an interval that uses a Key Signature, the sharps or flats in the Key Signature apply to all notes with that name (on the staff and on ledger lines).

So-La Says: When Chromatically Altering an Interval, the **Interval Quality** will change. The **Interval Number** will stay the same.

Chromatically Altering to become **Larger** = The distance in pitch between the 2 notes has increased.

Chromatically Altering to become **Smaller** = The distance in pitch between the 2 notes has decreased.

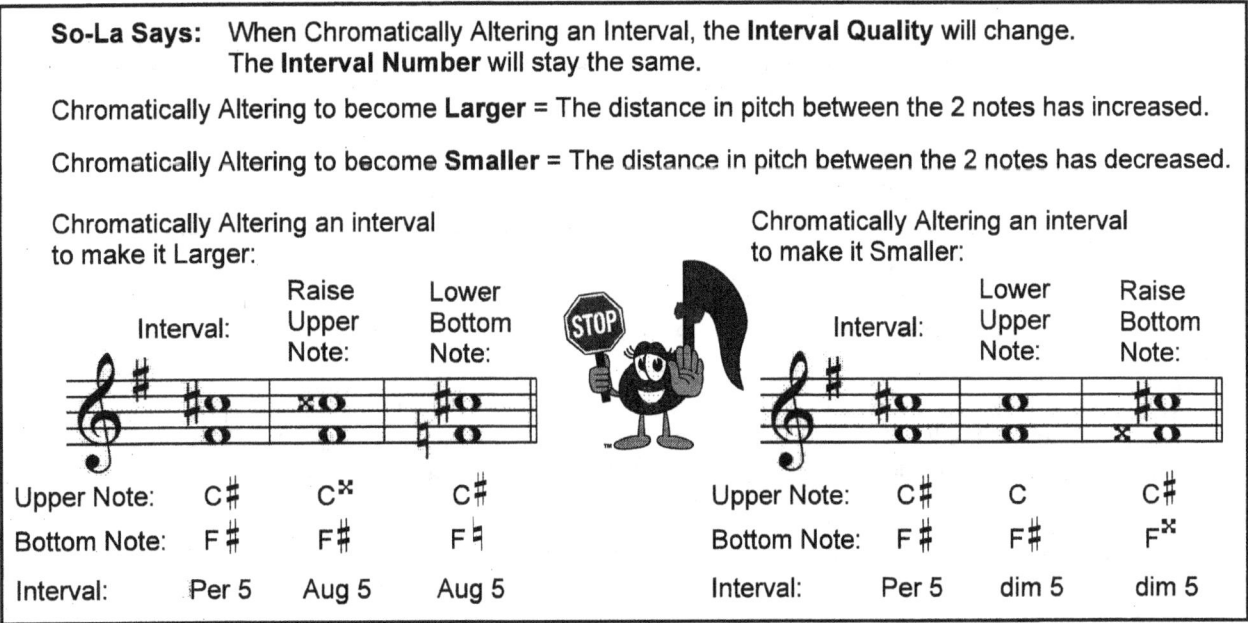

♪ **Ti-Do Tip:**

Chromatic Alteration	Original Interval		New Interval Quality
Half step (semitone) **smaller**:	Major	smaller	minor
- lower the upper (top) note;	minor	becomes	diminished
- raise the bottom note.	Augmented		Major or Perfect
	Perfect		diminished

When writing intervals using a Key Signature (with or without bar lines), **accidentals** may be required to raise or lower the chromatically altered note. Observe any bar lines when rewriting or altering intervals.

1. a) Name the given interval.
   b) Rewrite the interval, Chromatically Altering the interval to make it smaller by lowering the upper (top) note by a chromatic half step. Name the new interval.

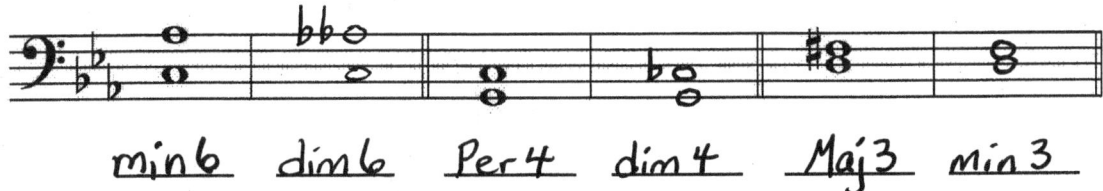

min 6   dim 6   Per 4   dim 4   Maj 3   min 3

2. a) Name the given interval.
   b) Rewrite the interval, Chromatically Altering the interval to make it smaller by raising the bottom note by a chromatic half step. Name the new interval.

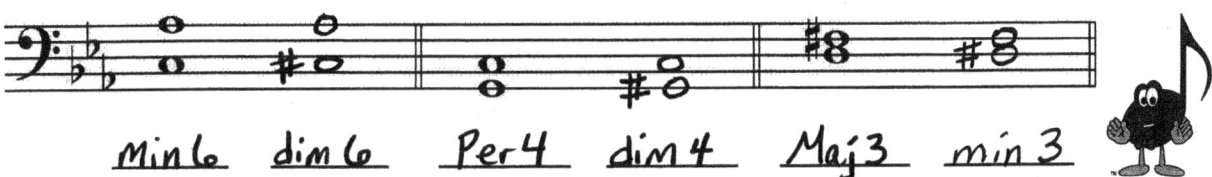

Min 6   dim 6   Per 4   dim 4   Maj 3   min 3

ENHARMONIC EQUIVALENT INTERVALS - Use after Intermediate Page 78

Enharmonic Equivalent Intervals are intervals that, when played, sound at the same pitch but are written using either a different upper (top) note or a different lower (bottom) note (an Enharmonic Equivalent).

Each key on the keyboard has at least 2 different names that may be written differently on the staff by using double sharps, sharps, naturals, flats and double flats. When selecting the Enharmonic Equivalent Note, it is important that the note selected will create an Interval Quality of Aug, Per, Maj, min or dim.

While intervals larger than an Augmented and smaller than a diminished are found in music (especially in Atonal Music), it is preferable at this level to use a **Standard Interval Quality** (Aug, Per, Maj, min or dim).

> **So-La Says:** When changing either the upper note **or** the lower note, an **Enharmonic Equivalent Interval** will have a different Number (1, 2, 3, etc.) and a different Quality (dim, min, Maj, Per or Aug) than the Original Interval.
>
> Step #1: On your Whiteboard, write the Enharmonic Equivalent Note Names for the upper (top) note or for the lower (bottom) note (according to the instructions in the Question).
> Step #2: Which note will allow you to make an acceptable Interval Quality? Write the answer.
>
> Question: Change the Upper Note Enharmonically.
>
> Step #1: Enharmonic Equivalent of B♭ = A♯ or C♭♭.
>
> Step #2: Which one is correct?
> F♯ to A♯ = Major 3
> F♯ to C♭♭ = ?? 5
>
> Answer: dim 4   Maj 3

1. a) Name the given interval.
   b) Rewrite the interval, changing the upper (top) note enharmonically. Name the new interval.

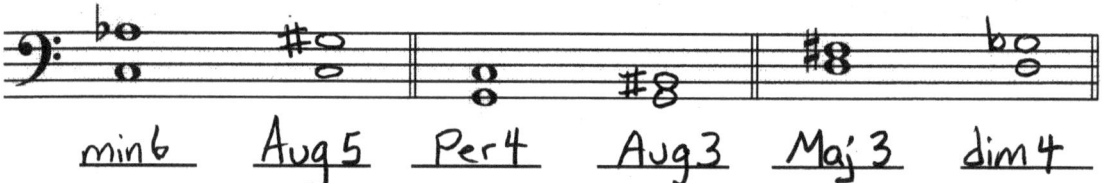

min 6   Aug 5   Per 4   Aug 3   Maj 3   dim 4

2. a) Name the given interval.
   b) Rewrite the interval, changing the lower (bottom) note enharmonically. Name the new interval.

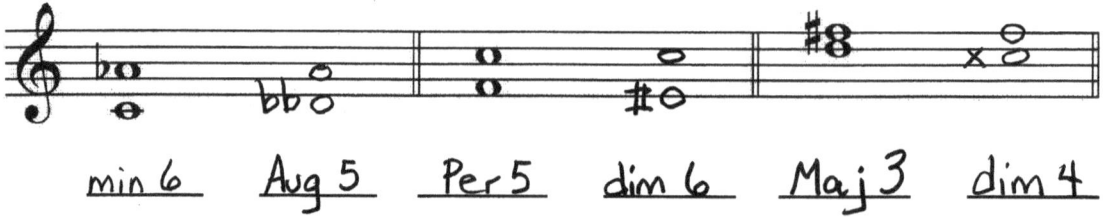

min 6   Aug 5   Per 5   dim 6   Maj 3   dim 4

> ♪ **Ti-Do Time:** Play each pair of intervals on Page 26. Listen. Do they sound at the same pitch? Can you hear any difference when you play each pair of intervals?

ROOT/QUALITY CHORD SYMBOLS - Use after Intermediate Page 87

Review Pages 33 to 41 of the **Ultimate Music Theory LEVEL 5 Supplemental Workbook**: Chords.

Root/Quality Chord Symbols use letters to indicate the Root and the Quality of the Triad.

Major Triad = Root of the Triad, written using an upper case letter. (F)
Minor Triad = Root of the Triad, written using an upper case letter with an "m" for minor. (Fm)

Functional Chord Symbols use Roman Numerals to show the scale degree on which the triad is built and the type or quality (Major or minor) of the triad.

Major Triad = upper case Roman Numeral. (IV)   Minor Triad = lower case Roman Numeral. (iv)

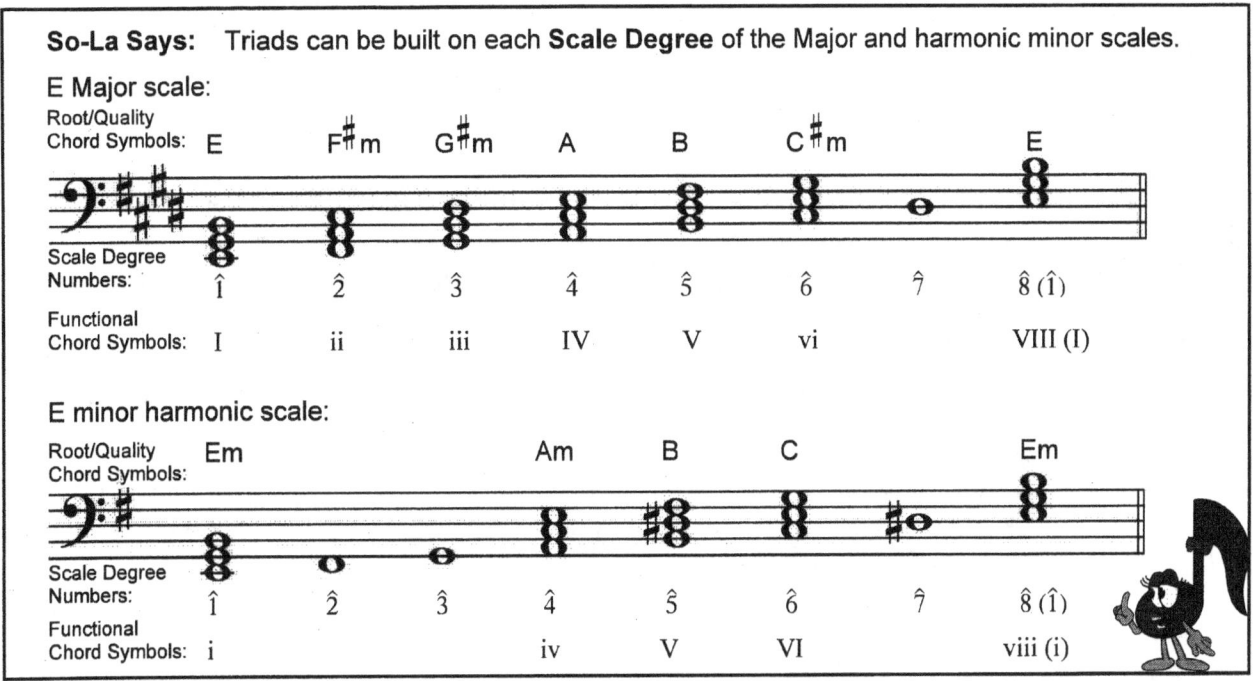

♪ **Ti-Do Tip:** At this Level, we are going to study only the Major and minor triads in each scale.

1. Add the Root/Quality Chord Symbol above each triad and the Functional Chord Symbol below.

a) D♭ Major scale:

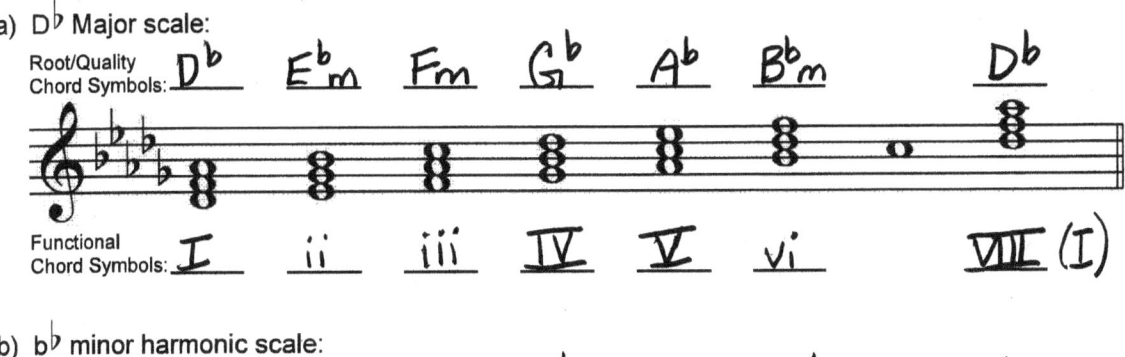

b) b♭ minor harmonic scale:

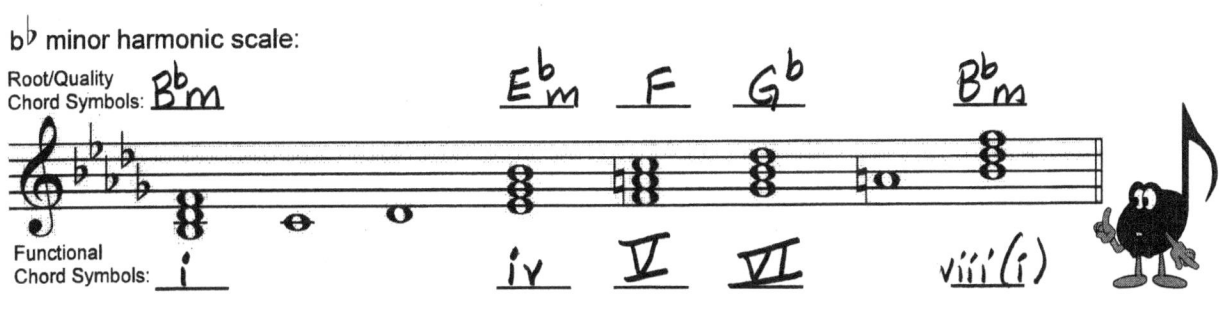

DOMINANT SEVENTH CHORDS - Use after Intermediate Page 89

The Dominant Seventh Chord (Dom 7 or V7) is a 4-note chord that is built on the fifth degree of a scale. The Dominant 7th Chord consists of a Root, Major 3, Perfect 5 and minor 7.

Review Pages 43 to 45 of the **Ultimate Music Theory LEVEL 5 Supplemental Workbook**: Dominant 7th Chords (including Root/Quality Chord Symbols, Functional Chord Symbols & Accidental Placement).

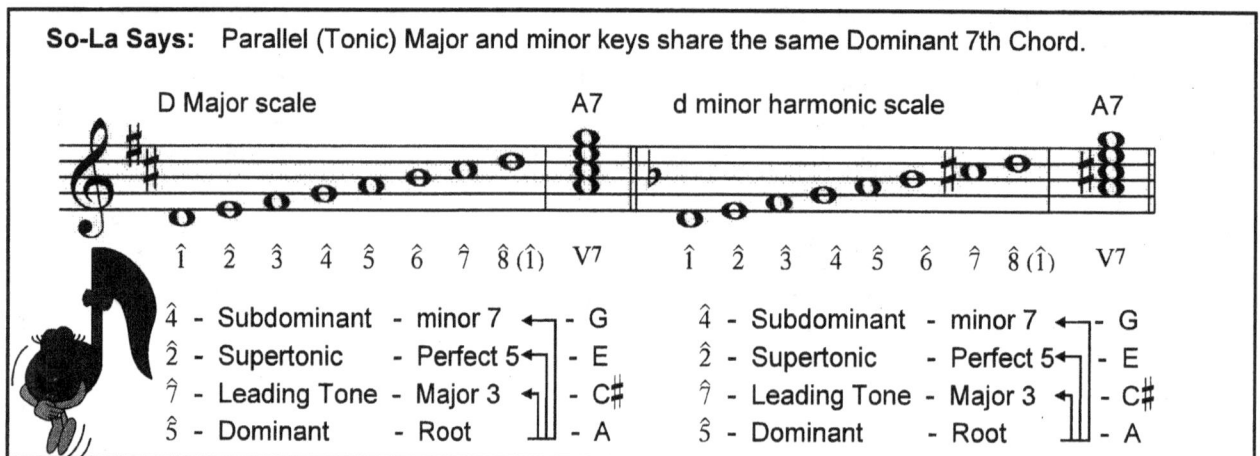

♫ **Ti-Do Tip:** The raised Leading Tone of the harmonic minor scale is always written with an accidental.

1. Following the example above:
    a) Write the ascending G Major scale in measure 1 and the Parallel (Tonic) g minor harmonic scale in measure 3. Use the correct Key Signatures and any necessary accidentals. Use whole notes.
    b) Write the Dominant Seventh Chords in measures 2 and 4.

2. Write the following root position Dominant Seventh Chords. Use the correct Key Signatures and any necessary accidentals. Use whole notes. Write the Root/Quality Chord Symbol above and the Functional Chord Symbol below each chord.
    a) Dominant Seventh Chord of F Major
    b) Dominant Seventh Chord of f minor
    c) Dominant Seventh Chord of C♯ Major
    d) Dominant Seventh Chord of c♯ minor

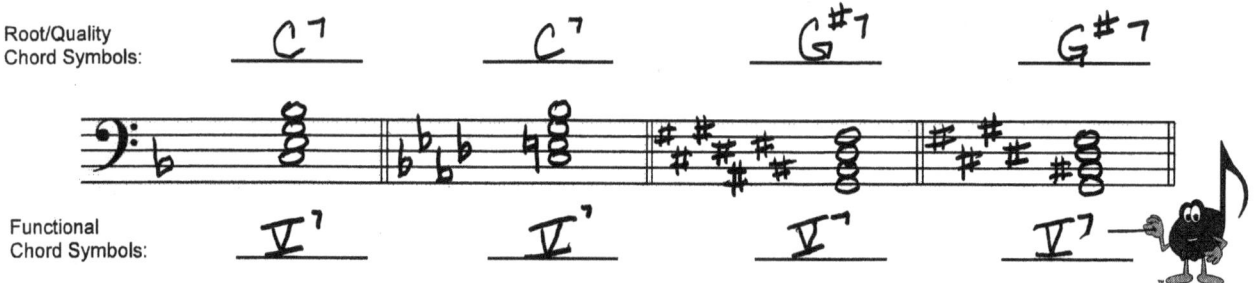

OPEN POSITION 4-PART CHORALE (SATB) TEXTURE - Use after Page 89

One type of 4-Part Texture is Chorale Style (or SATB) with 4 voices: Soprano, Alto, Tenor and Bass. In the UMT LEVEL 4 and LEVEL 5 you learned about vocal ranges for SATB and ranges for instruments.

The human voice may be categorized in a specific voice part (SATB). However, each human voice has its own tessitura. Tessitura is the range where the voice is most comfortable singing to produce its best vocal timbre and characteristic sound. A vocalist may expand their tessitura through vocal exercises and practice.

Average Vocal Ranges for **SATB**:   1. Write the notes for the average Vocal Ranges for SATB.

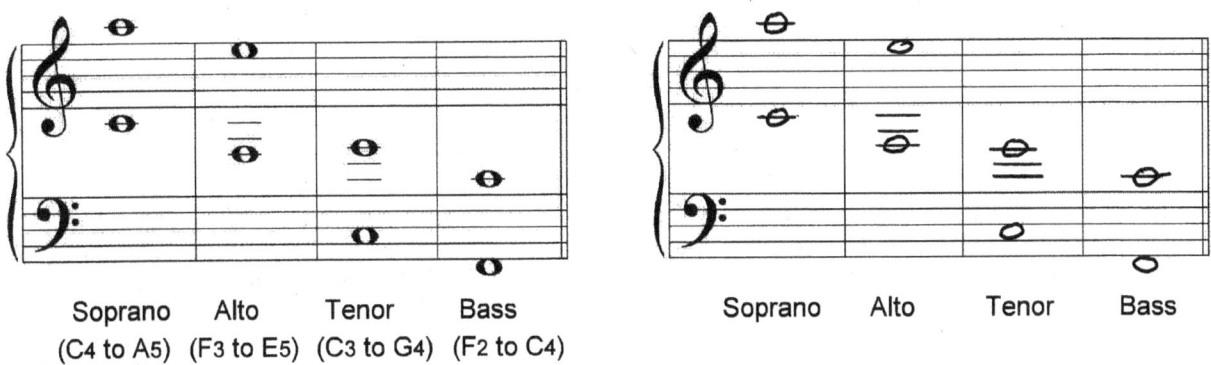

Soprano Alto Tenor Bass
(C4 to A5) (F3 to E5) (C3 to G4) (F2 to C4)

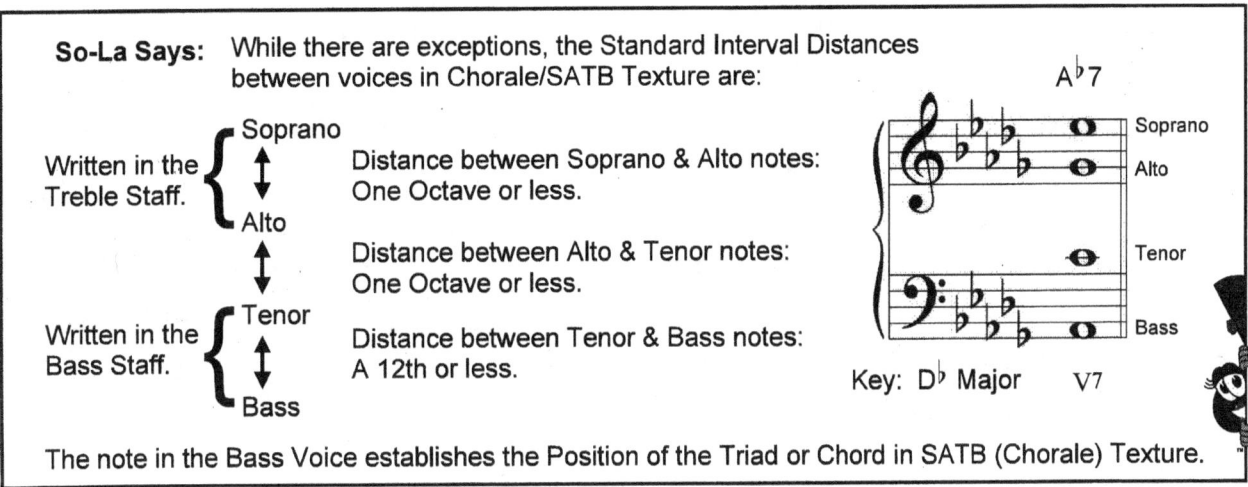

So-La Says: While there are exceptions, the Standard Interval Distances between voices in Chorale/SATB Texture are:

Written in the Treble Staff: Soprano ↕ Alto — Distance between Soprano & Alto notes: One Octave or less.

Distance between Alto & Tenor notes: One Octave or less.

Written in the Bass Staff: Tenor ↕ Bass — Distance between Tenor & Bass notes: A 12th or less.

Key: D♭ Major   V7

The note in the Bass Voice establishes the Position of the Triad or Chord in SATB (Chorale) Texture.

♪ **Ti-Do Tip:** The notes above the Bass note can be in any order, as long as they are within the Standard Interval Distances for each of the Voices in SATB (Chorale) Texture.

2. Add the notes in the Soprano, Alto and Tenor voices to complete each Dominant Seventh Chord in SATB (Chorale) Texture. Use whole notes. Use accidentals if needed. Observe the SATB Vocal Ranges and the Standard Interval Distances between the voices. (There will be more than one correct answer.)

Root/Quality Chord Symbols: C♯7   F7   B7   E♭7   A7

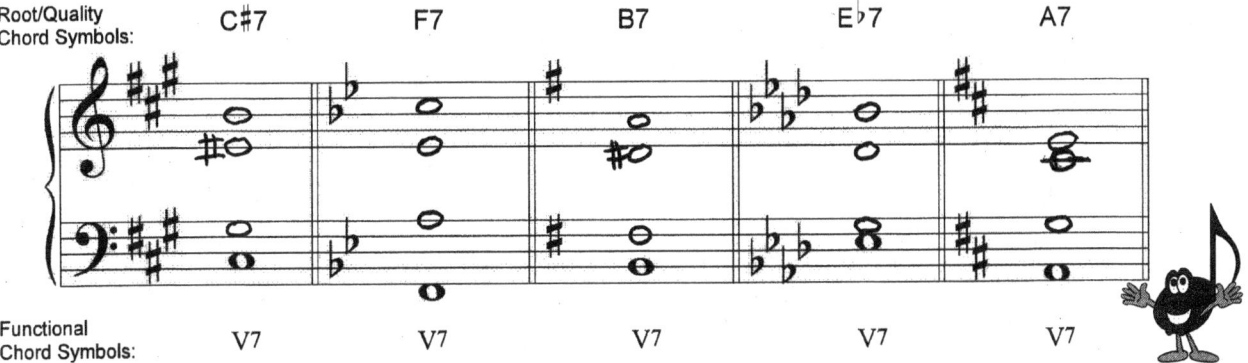

Functional Chord Symbols: V7   V7   V7   V7   V7

REWRITING OPEN to CLOSE POSITION TRIADS REVIEW - Use after Intermediate Page 89

It is important to have completed the **UMT Level 5 Supplemental Workbook** (page 46) to have a solid foundation in identifying triads in Close Position.

A triad in **Close Position** is written with notes as close together as possible. No interval is larger than a 6th.
A triad in **Open Position** is written with intervals that can be larger than a 6th.

When a triad is written in Open or Close Position, it can be written on one staff or on the Grand Staff.

A triad can also be written in **4-Part Chorale/SATB Texture**. Each part of a 4-Part Texture is called a **Voice**. A triad has only 3 notes, so when written in a 4-Part Texture, it will mean doubling one of the three notes. At this level, the easiest note to double is the root note (or the fifth note).

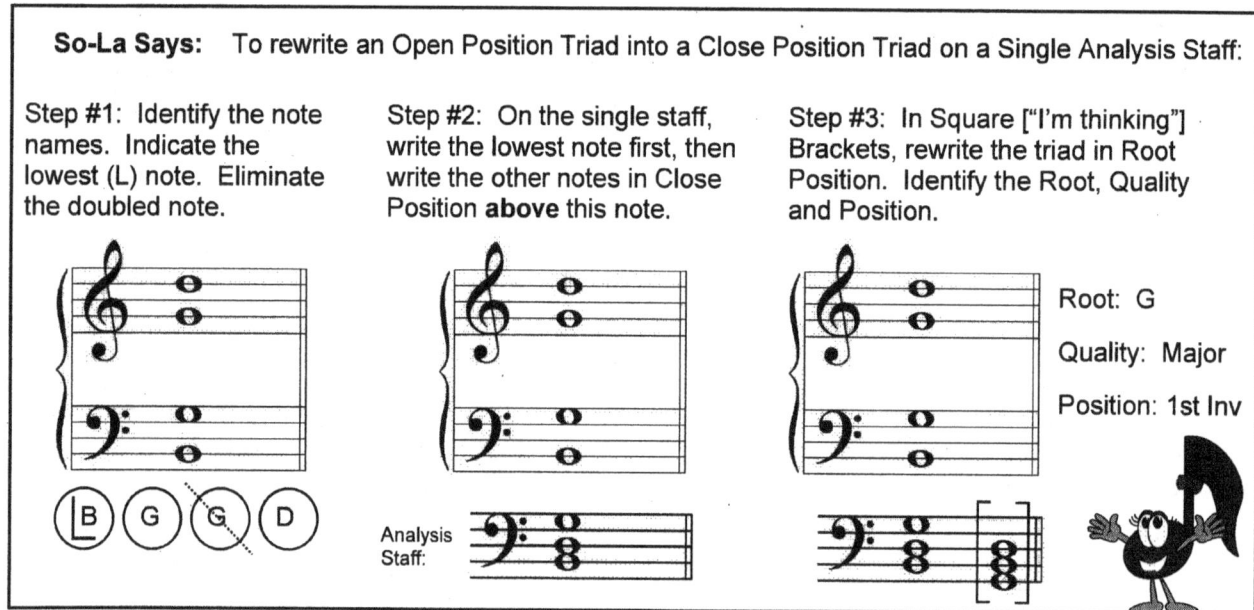

So-La Says: To rewrite an Open Position Triad into a Close Position Triad on a Single Analysis Staff:

Step #1: Identify the note names. Indicate the lowest (L) note. Eliminate the doubled note.

Step #2: On the single staff, write the lowest note first, then write the other notes in Close Position **above** this note.

Step #3: In Square ["I'm thinking"] Brackets, rewrite the triad in Root Position. Identify the Root, Quality and Position.

Root: G
Quality: Major
Position: 1st Inv

1. a) Identify the note names. Indicate the lowest note with the "L". Eliminate the doubled note.
   b) On the single staff, write the lowest note first, then write the other notes above in Close Position.
   c) Write the root position triad in the Square Brackets. Identify the Root, Quality and Position.

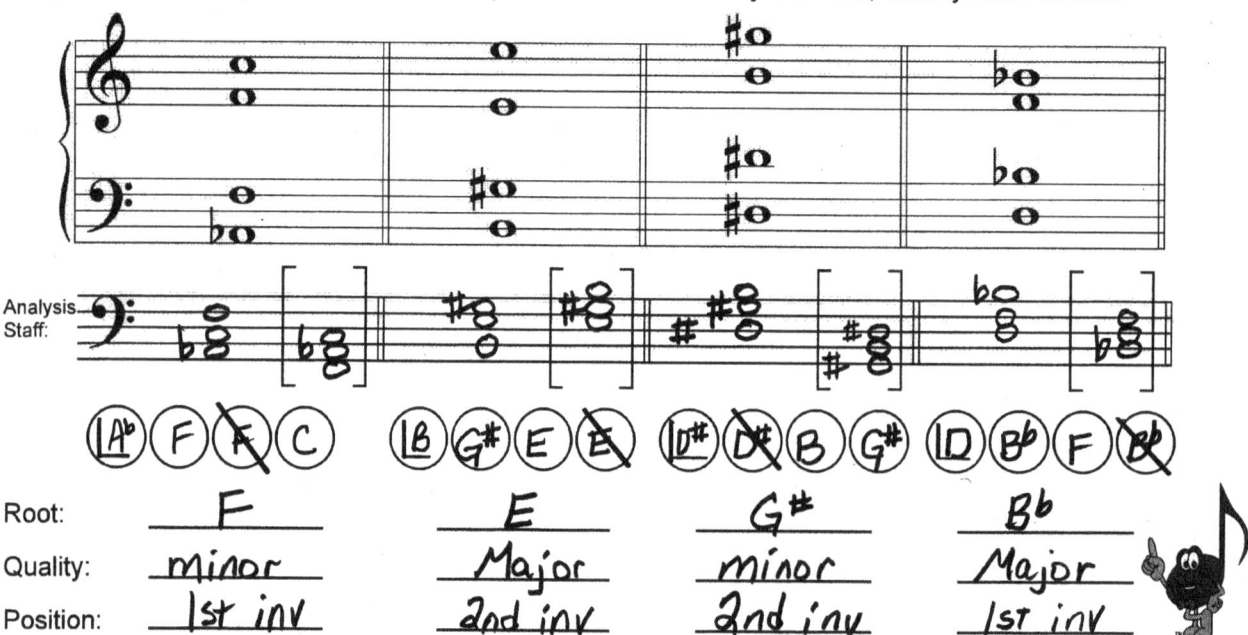

Root:	F	E	G#	Bb
Quality:	minor	Major	minor	Major
Position:	1st inv	2nd inv	2nd inv	1st inv

REWRITING CLOSE to OPEN POSITION TRIADS - Use after Intermediate Page 89

The lowest note of the Close or Open Position Triad establishes the **Position** (root pos, 1st inv or 2nd inv).

When rewriting a Close Position Triad into Open Position (or an Open Position Triad into Close Position), the lowest (bottom) note must remain the same.

- A Close Position Triad in root position will be rewritten in Open Position in root position;
- A Close Position Triad in first inversion will be rewritten in Open Position in first inversion;
- A Close Position Triad in second inversion will be rewritten in Open Position in second inversion.

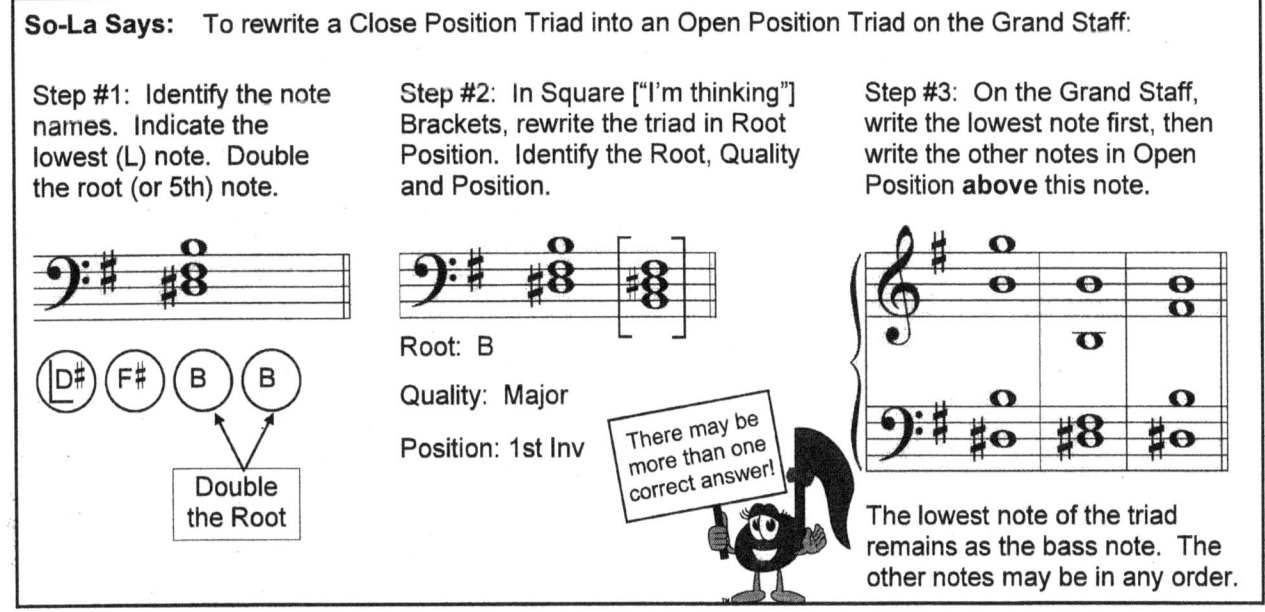

So-La Says: To rewrite a Close Position Triad into an Open Position Triad on the Grand Staff:

Step #1: Identify the note names. Indicate the lowest (L) note. Double the root (or 5th) note.

Step #2: In Square ["I'm thinking"] Brackets, rewrite the triad in Root Position. Identify the Root, Quality and Position.

Root: B
Quality: Major
Position: 1st Inv

There may be more than one correct answer!

Step #3: On the Grand Staff, write the lowest note first, then write the other notes in Open Position **above** this note.

The lowest note of the triad remains as the bass note. The other notes may be in any order.

♪ **Ti-Do Tip:** Observing the SATB Vocal Ranges and the Standard Interval Distances between the voices, there will be more than one correct answer.

1. a) Identify the note names. Indicate the lowest note with the "L". Double the root note.
   b) Write the root position triad in the Square Brackets. Identify the Root, Quality and Position.
   c) On the Grand Staff, write the lowest note first, then write the other notes above in Open Position.

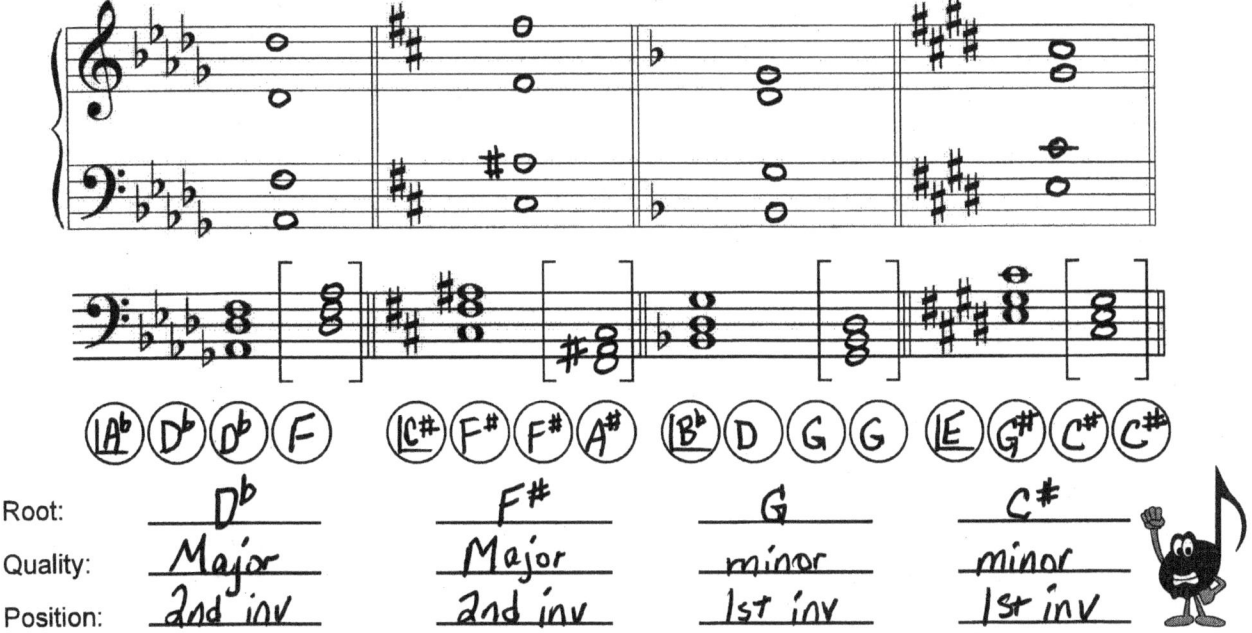

Root: D♭ / F♯ / G / C♯
Quality: Major / Major / minor / minor
Position: 2nd inv / 2nd inv / 1st inv / 1st inv

REWRITING OPEN to CLOSE POSITION DOMINANT SEVENTH CHORDS - Use after Page 89

Triads and Dominant Seventh Chords (in Open or in Close Position) may be written in **Complete** Form (all notes written at least once) or **Incomplete** Form (one note omitted).

Complete Triad: A triad with all notes (root, 3rd, 5th) written once. The root or 5th can also be doubled to create a 4-note Triad.

Complete Dominant Seventh Chord: A Dominant 7th Chord with all notes (root, 3rd, 5th, 7th) written once.

Incomplete Dominant Seventh Chord: The 5th is usually omitted and the root doubled (root, root, 3rd, 7th).

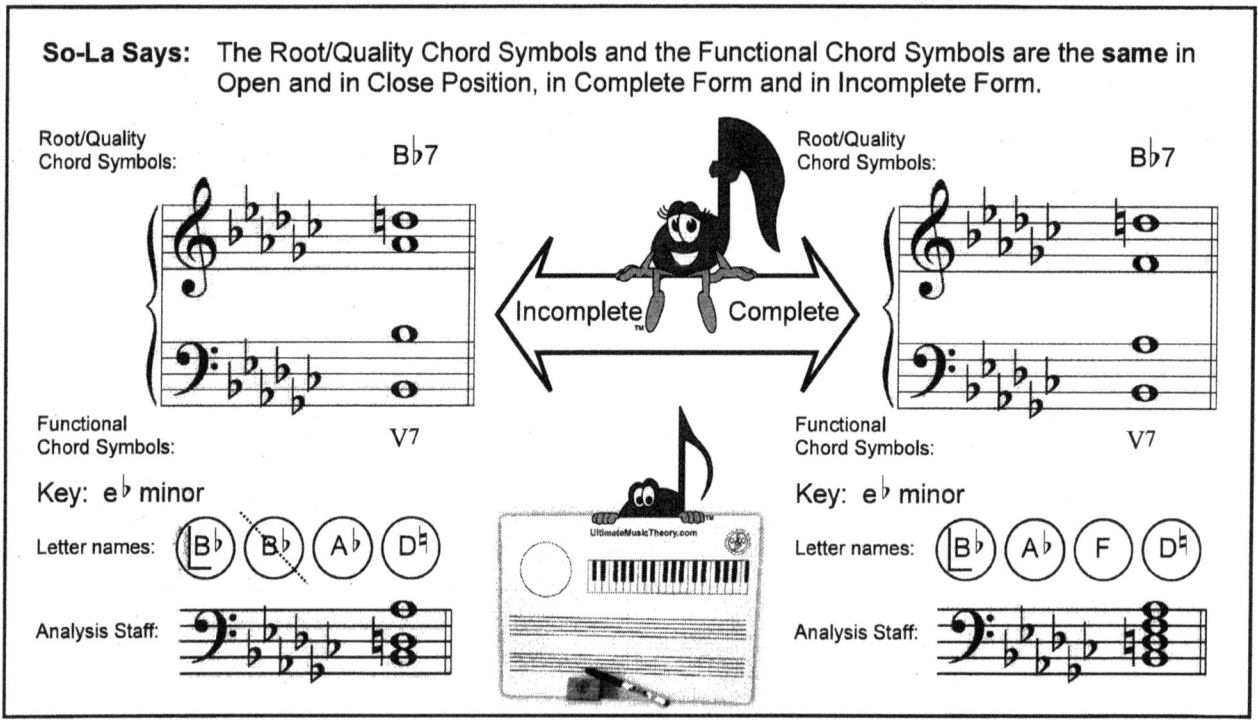

♫ **Ti-Do Tip:** When there is no room in the exercise to write the Letter Names, use your UMT Whiteboard.

1. a) Name the Major or minor key for each Open Position Dominant Seventh Chord.
   b) Rewrite each Open Position Dominant Seventh Chord in Close Position on the Analysis Staff.

REWRITING CLOSE to OPEN POSITION DOMINANT SEVENTH CHORDS - Use after Page 89

To rewrite a Dominant Seventh Chord from Close Position into **Open Position**:

Step #1: Identify the note names. Indicate the lowest (L) note.

Step #2: If the Dominant Seventh Chord is **Complete** (root, 3rd, 5th, 7th), no doubling will be needed. If the Dominant Seventh Chord is **Incomplete**, the root will be doubled (root, root, 3rd, 7th).

Step #3: On the Grand Staff, write the root note as the lowest note, then write the other notes in Open Position above this note. Observe the SATB Vocal Ranges and the Standard Interval Distances between the voices. (There will be more than one correct answer.)

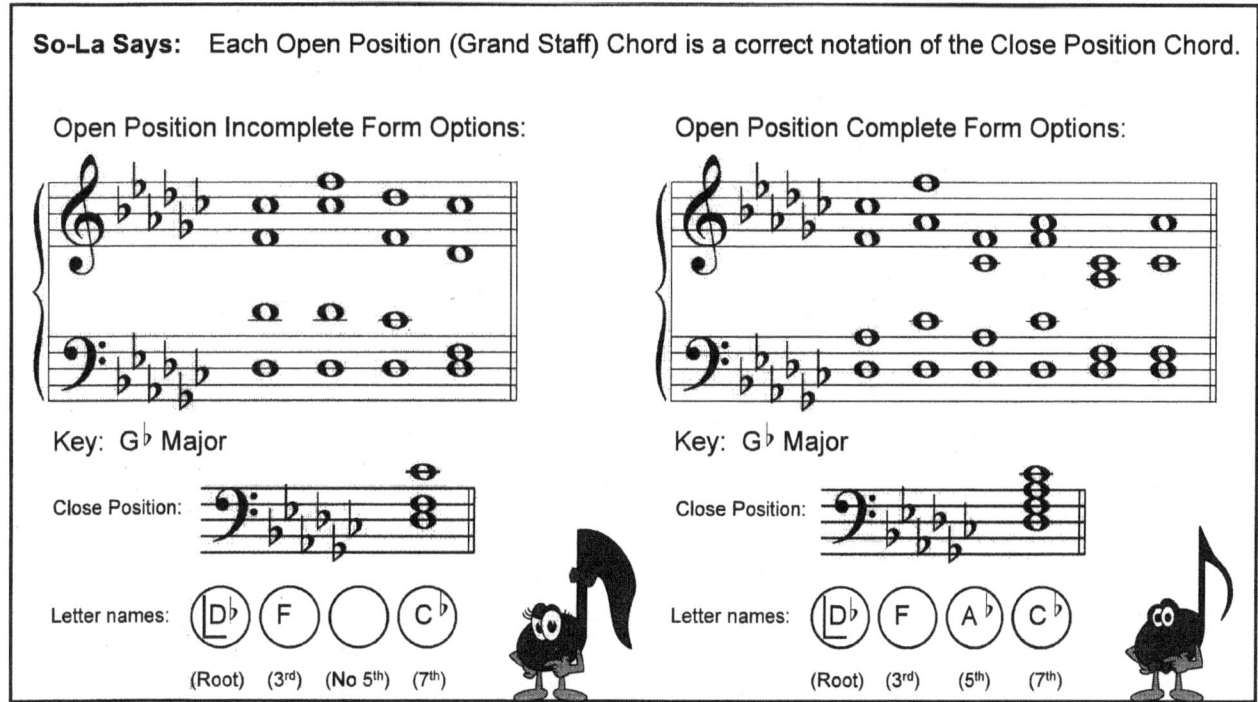

♫ **Ti-Do Tip:** When there is no room in the exercise to write the Letter Names, use your UMT Whiteboard.

1. a) Name the Major or minor key for each Close Position Dominant Seventh Chord.
   b) Following the Steps, rewrite each Close Position V7 Chord in Open Position on the Grand Staff.

TRIADS and CHORDS - OPEN to CLOSE REVIEW - Use after Intermediate Page 89

The Quality (Type) of a Triad is either Major (Root - Major 3 - Perfect 5) or minor (Root - minor 3 - Perfect 5).
The Quality of a Dominant 7th Chord (Root - Major 3 - Perfect 5 - minor 7) is simply Dominant 7th (Dom 7th).

So-La Says: When written with **Accidentals**, a Dominant Seventh Chord will belong to **both** the Major and Parallel (Tonic) minor keys.

When written with a **Key Signature**, a Dominant Seventh Chord will belong to **either** the Major or Relative minor key.

♪ **Ti-Do Tip:** A Dominant 7th Chord can be Complete (all notes) or Incomplete (missing 5th, doubled root).

1. a) Rewrite each Dominant Seventh Chord in Close Position in the Single Treble Staff below.
   b) Name the Major and the minor keys to which each Dominant Seventh Chord belongs.
   c) Write the Root/Quality Chord Symbol above the Grand Staff for each Dominant Seventh Chord.

2. a) Identify the Root, Quality (Maj, min, Dom 7th) and Position (root pos, 1st inv, 2nd inv) for each chord.
   b) Write the Root/Quality Chord Symbol above each Chord.

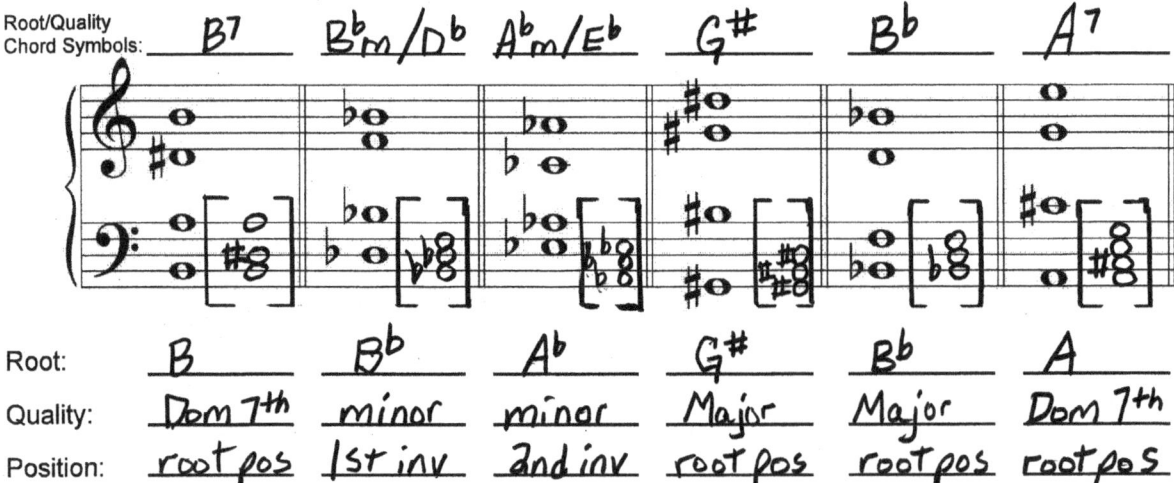

IMPLIED HARMONY - HARMONIC ANALYSIS of BROKEN TRIADS/CHORDS - Use after Page 89

Harmonic Analysis is the process of naming the triads and chords in relationship to the key. Triads and chords can be written in Complete (all notes written at least once) or Incomplete Form (one note omitted).

Root/Quality Chord Symbols identify the Root, the Quality and the lowest note (the Slash = an inversion).
At this level, Triads will be analyzed in root position (G), first inversion (G/B) or second inversion (G/D).
At this level, the Dominant Seventh Chords will be analyzed in root position (G7) only.

Functional Chord Symbols identify the Root, the Quality and the Scale Degree. (The added Figured Bass, written after the Roman Numeral, indicates the Position of the triad.)
At this level, Triads will be analyzed in root position (V or V^5_3), first inversion (V^6_3) or second inversion (V^6_4).
At this level, the Dominant Seventh Chord will be analyzed in root position (V7) only.

Melodies can "**imply**" (or suggest) a harmony (chordal accompaniment) through the choice of notes used in the Monophonic Texture of the melody. Chords "implied by the melody" refer to the chords that could be played along with the melody to create a Homophonic Texture.

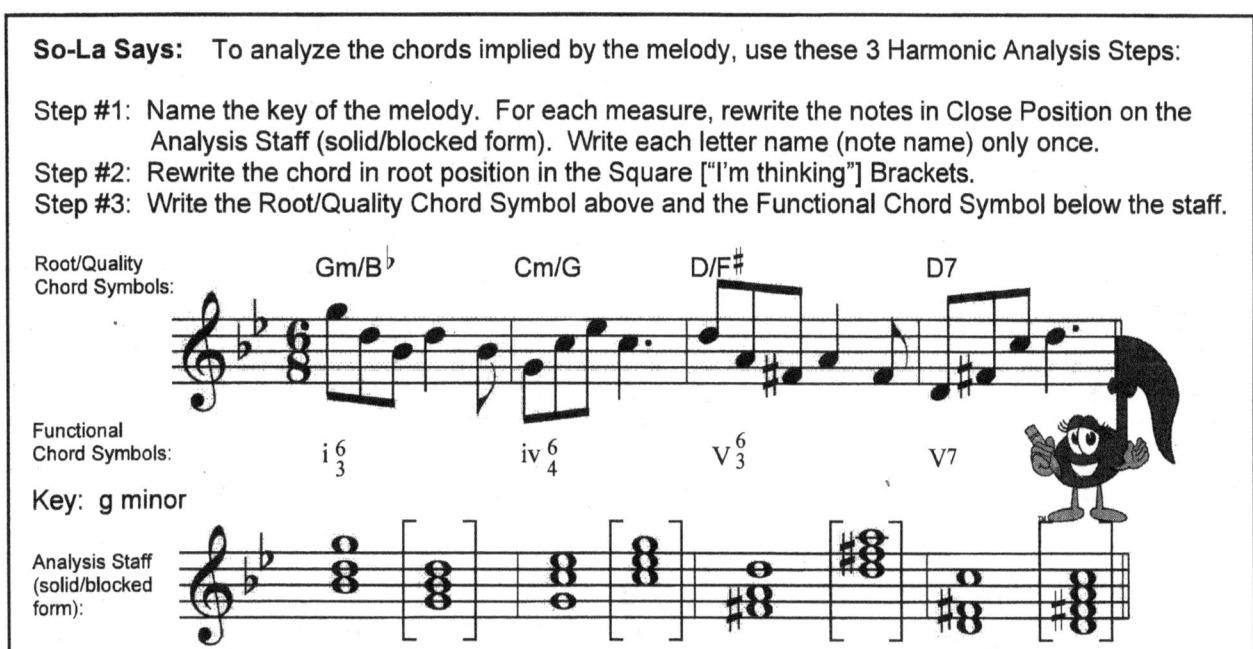

So-La Says: To analyze the chords implied by the melody, use these 3 Harmonic Analysis Steps:

Step #1: Name the key of the melody. For each measure, rewrite the notes in Close Position on the Analysis Staff (solid/blocked form). Write each letter name (note name) only once.
Step #2: Rewrite the chord in root position in the Square ["I'm thinking"] Brackets.
Step #3: Write the Root/Quality Chord Symbol above and the Functional Chord Symbol below the staff.

1. Name the key of the melody. Use the Harmonic Analysis Steps to write the Root/Quality Chord Symbols (implied by the melody) above each measure and the Functional Chord Symbols below each measure.

MUSICAL EXCERPT ANALYSIS on a GRAND STAFF - Use after Intermediate Page 89

Composers use different textures, forms and positions when writing music. When analyzing a **Musical Excerpt** from a composition written on the Grand Staff, triads and chords can be written in Open or Closed Position, in Solid/Blocked or Broken Form with notes (in any order) throughout both staves.

So-La Says: To make analysis on a Grand Staff easy, use the **3 Musical Excerpt Analysis Steps**:

Step #1: Identify the key of the excerpt. For each measure, rewrite the notes in Close Position on the Analysis Staff (solid/blocked form). Write each letter name (note name) only once.
Step #2: If not in root position, rewrite the chord in root position in Square ["I'm thinking"] Brackets.
Step #3: Name the Root, the Quality (Maj, min or Dom 7) and the Position (root pos, 1st inv or 2nd inv).

The following excerpt is from Johann Philipp Kirnberger's "Les carillons".

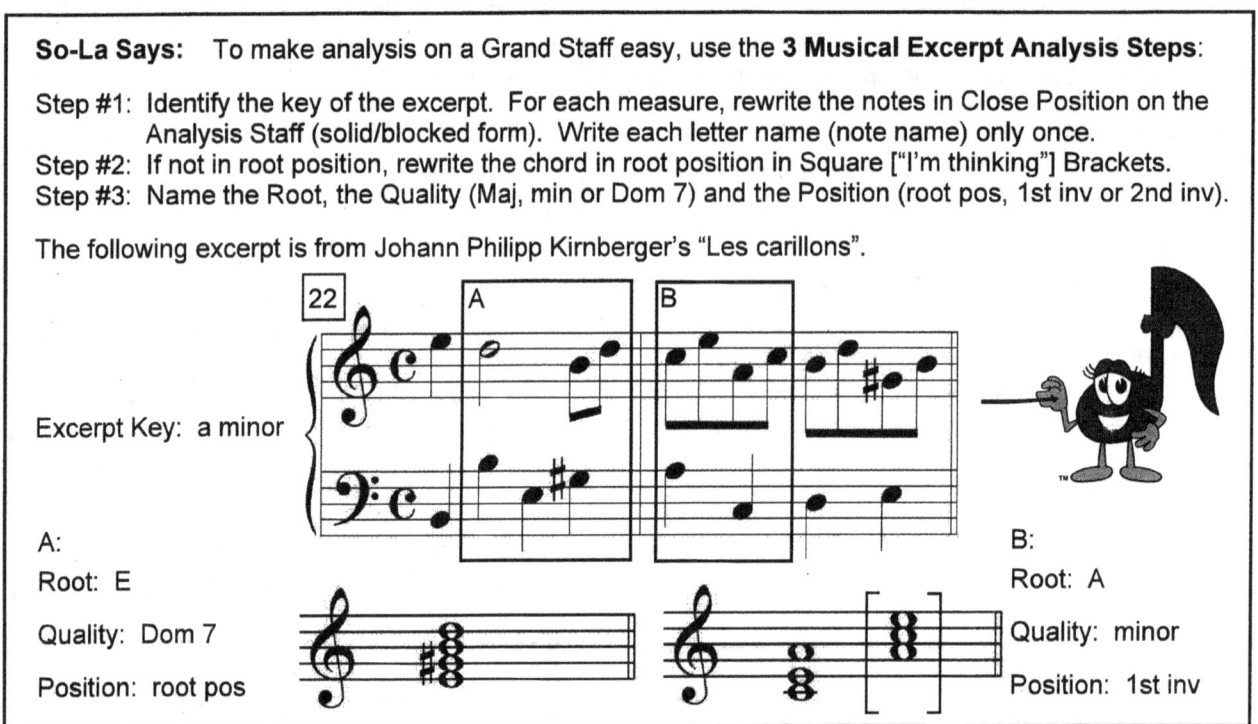

Excerpt Key: a minor

A:
Root: E
Quality: Dom 7
Position: root pos

B:
Root: A
Quality: minor
Position: 1st inv

"Les carillons" begins in A Major, then modulates through other keys (including a minor, C Major, c minor, E Major and e minor). It also starts in ¢ Time, then changes to C Time.

1. These measures are from J.P. Kirnberger's "Les carillons". Follow the 3 Musical Excerpt Analysis Steps to: identify the key of the musical excerpt and, for the chords, name the: Root, Quality and Position.

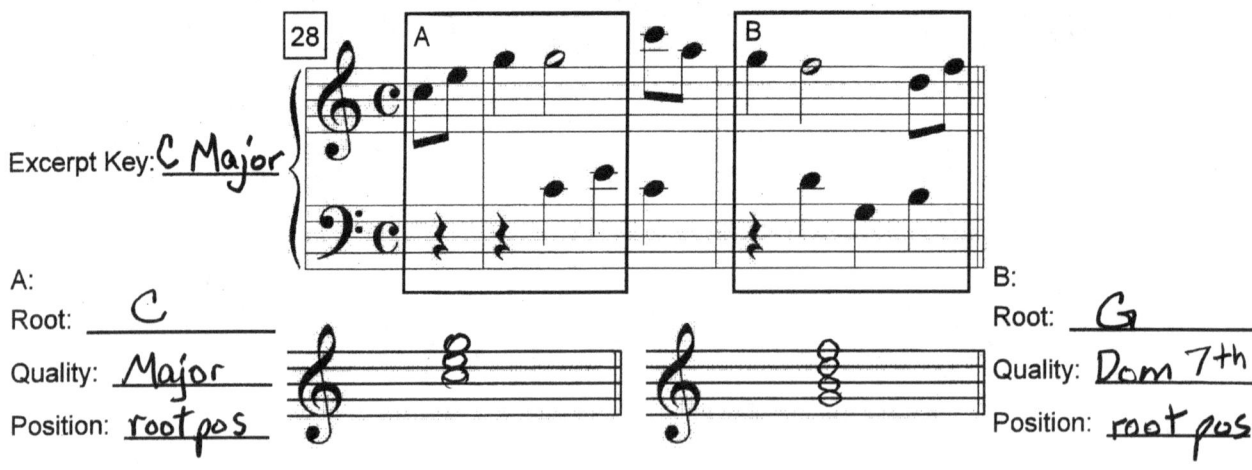

Excerpt Key: C Major

A:
Root: C
Quality: Major
Position: root pos

B:
Root: G
Quality: Dom 7th
Position: root pos

♫ **Ti-Do Time:** Play each Musical Excerpt on your instrument.
Your Teacher will then play one of the Musical Excerpts. Can you identify whether it is the C Major excerpt or the a minor excerpt?

ALBERTI BASS - BROKEN CHORD PATTERN - Use after Intermediate Page 89

A melody may have a harmonic accompaniment of solid or broken chords. An **Alberti bass** is a simple repeated pattern of alternating notes of broken chords (usually in the Bass) on which the harmony is based.

Alberti bass was named after Italian composer Domenico Alberti (1710 - 1740), although he did not invent it. This form was popular for harpsichord and early piano music as a way to extend the sound of a chord since tones (sounds) on early keyboard instruments faded quickly. Mozart used Alberti bass in his piano sonatas.

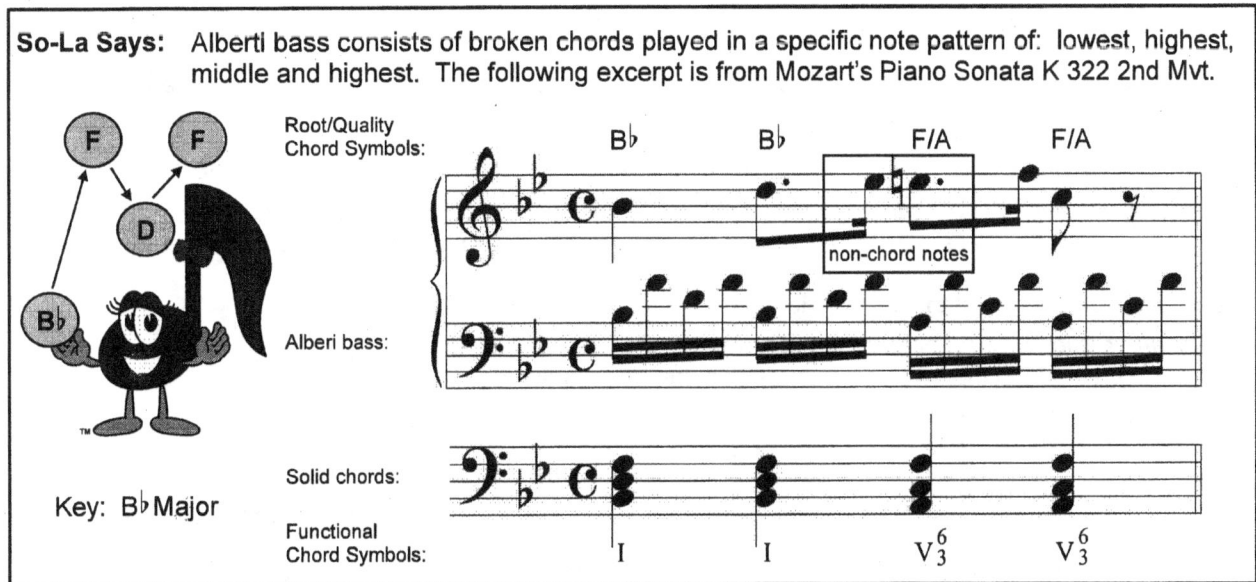

1. Write the Root/Quality Chord Symbol above each solid chord. Name the notes of each Alberti bass directly below each note.

2. Write the Functional Chord Symbol below each solid chord. On the staff directly below each measure, rewrite each solid chord as an Alberti bass (lowest, highest, middle and highest). Use eighth notes.

ITALIAN TERMS and DEFINITIONS - Use after Intermediate Page 99

Italian "Prepositional" Terms are often used in front of **Italian "Noun/Pronoun" Terms** to create a descriptive direction for the performer:

Prepositional Terms: *con* - with; *senza* - without.
Noun/Pronoun Terms: *brio* - vigor; *fuoco* - fire; *grazia* - grace.

con brio - with vigor; *senza brio* - without vigor
con fuoco - with fire; *senza fuoco* - without fire
con grazia - with grace; *senza grazia* - without grace

Italian Terms may be combined by adding one term before or after another term. Each term has its own definition. Combinations of more than one term may be used to alter or create different meanings.

subito - "suddenly"; *molto* - "very"; *spiritoso* - "spirited" = *subito molto spiritoso* - suddenly very spirited

poco - "little"; *più* - "more"; *mosso* - "movement" = *poco più mosso* - little more movement
poco - "little"; *meno* - "less"; *mosso* - "movement" = *poco meno mosso* - little less movement

Other Italian Terms used at this level include:

ad libitum, ad lib. - at the liberty of the performer
simile - to continue in the same manner as has just been indicated

primo, prima - first; the upper part of a duet
secondo, seconda - second; the second or lower part of a duet

The dynamic **sforzando** - a sudden strong accent of a single note or chord - is indicated by  or .

So-La Says: Review the Musical Terms, Definitions and Signs in the Intermediate Rudiments Workbook:

Articulation, Signs, Terms, Tempo, Changes in Tempo, Dynamics and Stylistic (Style in Performance).

1. Explain the meaning of the combined Italian Terms below.

coll' ottava	with an added octave
poco a poco diminuendo	little by little becoming softer
meno espressivo	less expressive
subito allegretto e con grazia	suddenly fairly fast and with grace
mezzo forte e andantino	moderately loud and a little faster than andante
con grazia ed poco espressivo	with grace and little expression
con fuoco ed con moto	with fire and with movement
ben marcato e animato	well marked and animated
sempre senza pedale	always without pedal

REWRITING A MELODY and LEAD SHEETS - Use after Intermediate Page 109

Rewriting a melody using a Key Signature (and any necessary accidentals) includes rewriting all notation.

When rewriting a melody with chords, chord symbols may be used rather than chord notation. **Lead Sheets** are a form of written music where the Root/Quality Chord Symbols are written above the staff to indicate the chord structure accompaniment. Chords indicated may be played solid, broken, Alberti bass or improvised.

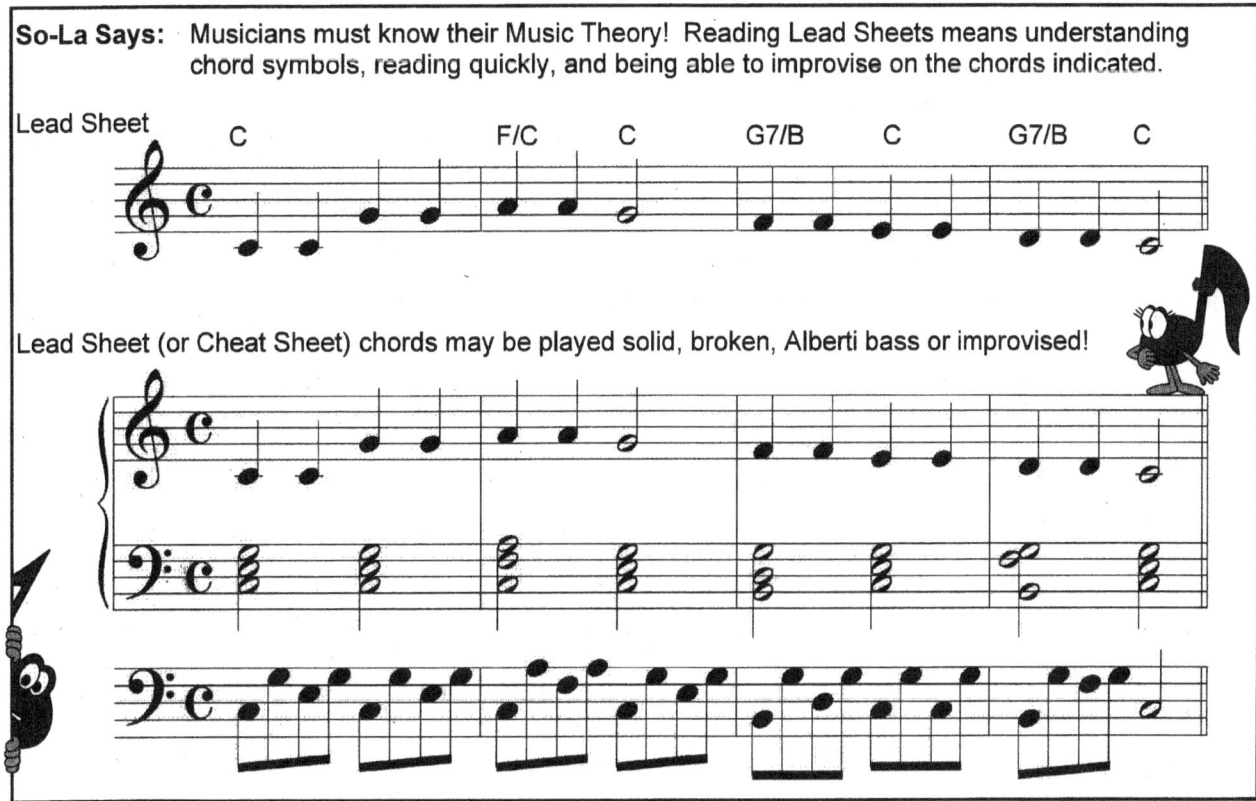

So-La Says: Musicians must know their Music Theory! Reading Lead Sheets means understanding chord symbols, reading quickly, and being able to improvise on the chords indicated.

Lead Sheet (or Cheat Sheet) chords may be played solid, broken, Alberti bass or improvised!

1. Rewrite the following melody using a Key Signature. Rewrite the chords as Functional Chord Symbols above each measure to create a Lead Sheet. Play the music using the Lead Sheet. Improvise!

REVIEW - AUTHENTIC and HALF CADENCES - Use after Intermediate Page 118

A **Cadence** is a progression of two (or more) chords used as "punctuation" at the end of a phrase.

A **Half Cadence** or Imperfect Cadence is a I (i) -V or IV (iv) -V cadence with the Root of each Chord written in the Bass Clef (lowest note). The top voice in Chord V ends on an unstable scale degree $\hat{5}$, $\hat{7}$ or $\hat{2}$ and is written in the Treble Clef (highest note). It sounds unfinished, like a question at the end of a sentence.

An **Authentic Cadence** or Perfect Cadence is a V - I (i) or V7 - I (i) cadence with the Root of each Chord written in the Bass Clef (lowest note). The top voice in Chord I ends on stable scale degree $\hat{1}$, $\hat{3}$ or $\hat{5}$ and is written in the Treble Clef (highest note). It sounds finished, like a period at the end of a sentence.

A **Perfect Authentic Cadence**, known as (PAC), is the same as an Authentic Cadence except that the top voice in Chord I MUST end on stable scale degree $\hat{1}$ (Tonic) and is written in the Treble Clef (highest note).

So-La Says: Follow the 3 Steps to create a Cadence Identification Chart to identify the Key & Cadence.

Step #1: Write the Major and relative minor keys for the given Key Signature.
Step #2: Identify the Tonic, Subdominant and Dominant Notes for each Key Signature.
Step #3: Match the Bass Notes in your Cadence Identification Chart to identify the Cadence Type.

Cadence Identification Chart:
B Major: I - B; IV - E; V - F#.
g# minor: i - G#; iv - C#; V - D#.
Bass Notes in Cadence: F# - B.

Look! The Bass Notes are only in the B Major Key: V (F#) and I (B).

No room to write a Cadence Identification Chart? Use your UMT Whiteboard!

Key: __B Major__
Cadence: __Authentic Cadence__

1. Complete the Cadence Identification Chart. Identify the Key and Cadence Type for each cadence.

a) Cadence Identification Chart:
__D♭__ Major: I - __D♭__; IV - __G♭__; V - __A♭__.
__b♭__ minor: i - __B♭__; iv - __E♭__; V - __F__.
Bass Notes in Cadence: __B♭__ - __F__.

Key: __b♭ minor__ i V
Cadence: __Half Cadence__

b) Cadence Identification Chart:
__A__ Major: I - __A__; IV - __D__; V - __E__.
__f#__ minor: i - __F#__; iv - __B__; V - __C#__.
Bass Notes in Cadence: __D__ - __E__.

Key: __A Major__ IV V
Cadence: __Half Cadence__

REVIEW - CADENCE IDENTIFICATION on the GRAND STAFF - Use after Intermediate Page 118

The Position of a Triad or Chord is based on the bottom (lowest) note. In a Cadence at this level, the bottom (lowest) note will be the root of each chord - the single note that is written in the Bass Clef.

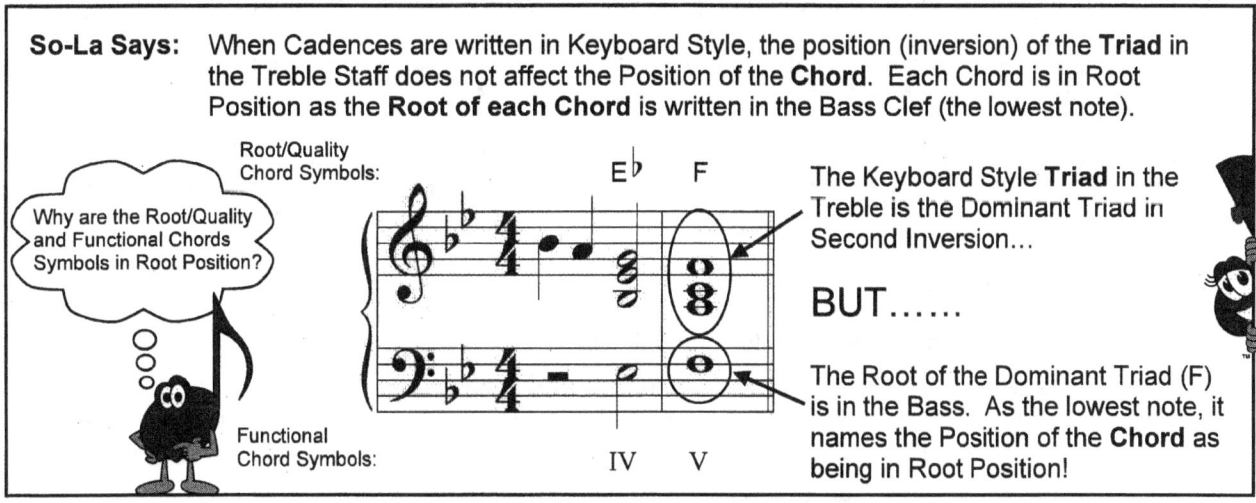

1. Name the key. Write the Root/Quality Chord Symbol above and the Functional Chord Symbol below each chord. Name the type of Cadence (Authentic or Half).

a) Root/Quality Chord Symbols: **B♭m F** 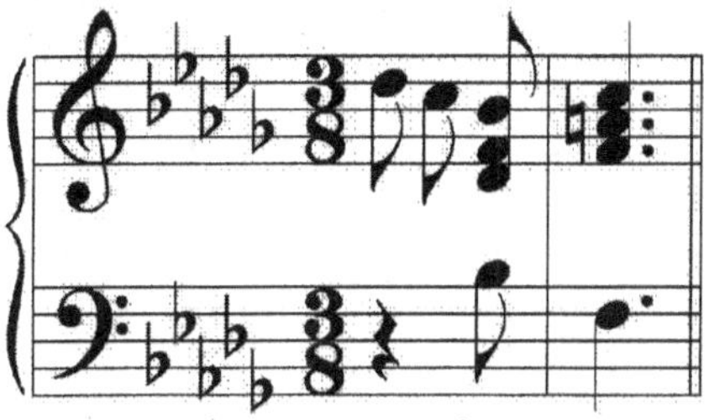
   Functional Chord Symbols: **i V**
   Key: **b♭ minor**
   Cadence: **Half Cadence**

b) Root/Quality Chord Symbols: **F# Bm** 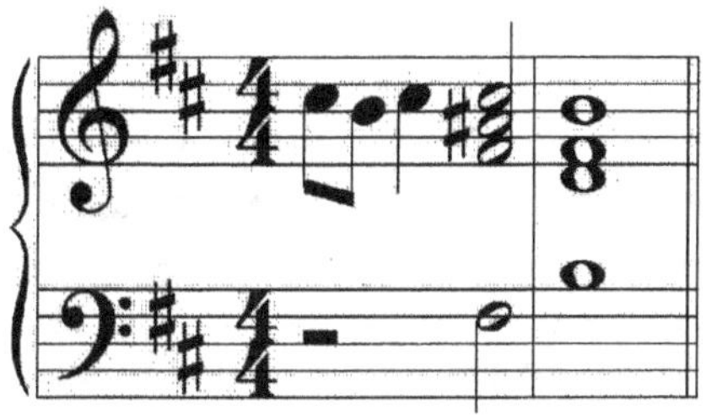
   Functional Chord Symbols: **V i**
   Key: **b minor**
   Cadence: **Authentic Cadence**

c) Root/Quality Chord Symbols: **B♭ C** 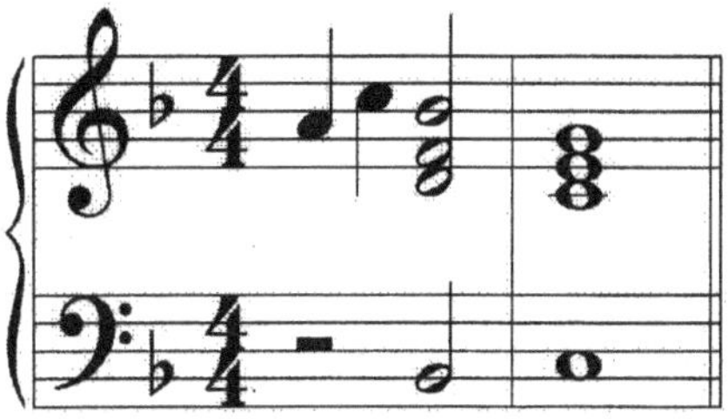
   Functional Chord Symbols: **IV V**
   Key: **F Major**
   Cadence: **Half Cadence**

d) Root/Quality Chord Symbols: **E♭ A♭** 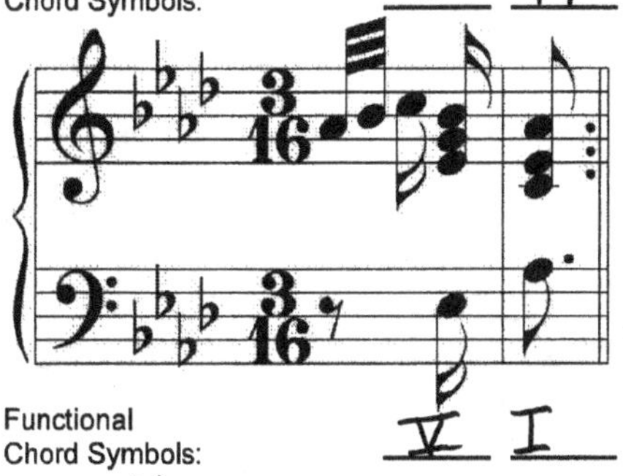
   Functional Chord Symbols: **V I**
   Key: **A♭ Major**
   Cadence: **Authentic Cadence**

TRANSPOSITION and MODULATION - Use after Intermediate Page 126

Transposition can be defined as rewriting music at a different pitch. In transposition, if the notes are moved by the exact same intervals, the music will be in a new key. The transposed music will sound exactly like the original except at a different pitch. Music in a Major key stays Major; music in a minor key stays minor.

Modulation occurs when the music shifts from one key to another. One way to modulate from one key to another is by using a common triad to "**bridge**" between the keys. Modulation creates variety and interest.

Music may begin in one key (the **Tonal Center** or the "Tonic") and then modulate a section/motive/phrase into another Tonal Center. Music in a Major key may modulate into a different Major or minor key. Music in a minor key may modulate into a different minor or Major key.

In "Harmonic Analysis" terms, modulation to a different/new key is confirmed with a Perfect Authentic (V - I or V - i) Cadence in the new key. Generally, if the music uses accidentals to create a new "Tonic", the music is considered to have modulated into (or "through") that key.

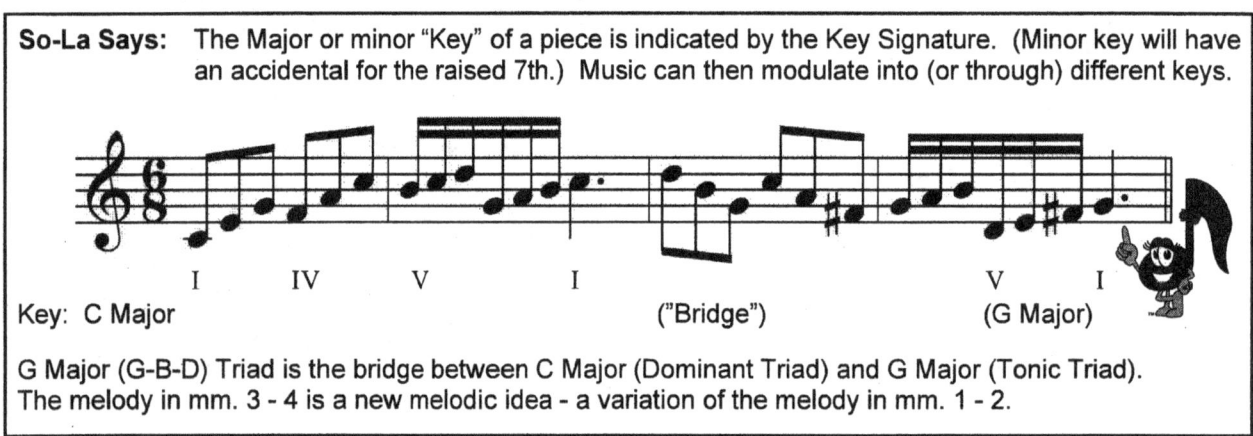

So-La Says: The Major or minor "Key" of a piece is indicated by the Key Signature. (Minor key will have an accidental for the raised 7th.) Music can then modulate into (or through) different keys.

Key: C Major   ("Bridge")   (G Major)

G Major (G-B-D) Triad is the bridge between C Major (Dominant Triad) and G Major (Tonic Triad). The melody in mm. 3 - 4 is a new melodic idea - a variation of the melody in mm. 1 - 2.

♫ **Ti-Do Tip:** A piece of music can modulate into a new key using the **same melody** (transposed into a different key) or a **new melodic idea** to create variation (new key/melody).

1. a) Identify the Key at the beginning of the melody and the new Key Modulation in the (brackets).
   b) Circle if the new modulation (mm. 3 - 4) is either a Transposition of the Melody or a New Melodic Idea.

a) Key: __E♭__ Major   (__B♭__ Major)

b) Circle if measures 3 - 4 is a: Transposition of the Melody   or   (New Melodic Idea.)

a) Key: __D__ Major   (__E__ Major)

b) Circle if measures 3 - 4 is a: (Transposition of the Melody)   or   New Melodic Idea.

MODULATION in MUSIC - Use after Intermediate Page 126

Modulation in Music - Composers in the Baroque (J.S. Bach) and Classical (W.A. Mozart) Period liked to modulate through different keys in a piece of music. This gave the music a sense of direction - a forward motion that provided the ability to repeat the original motives in different keys to create variety.

Modulation is a shift from one key to another, usually accomplished by moving through chord(s) shared by both keys, allowing smooth passage between the keys. The common chords create a "**bridge**" (a small section of music) that blends the old key into the new key.

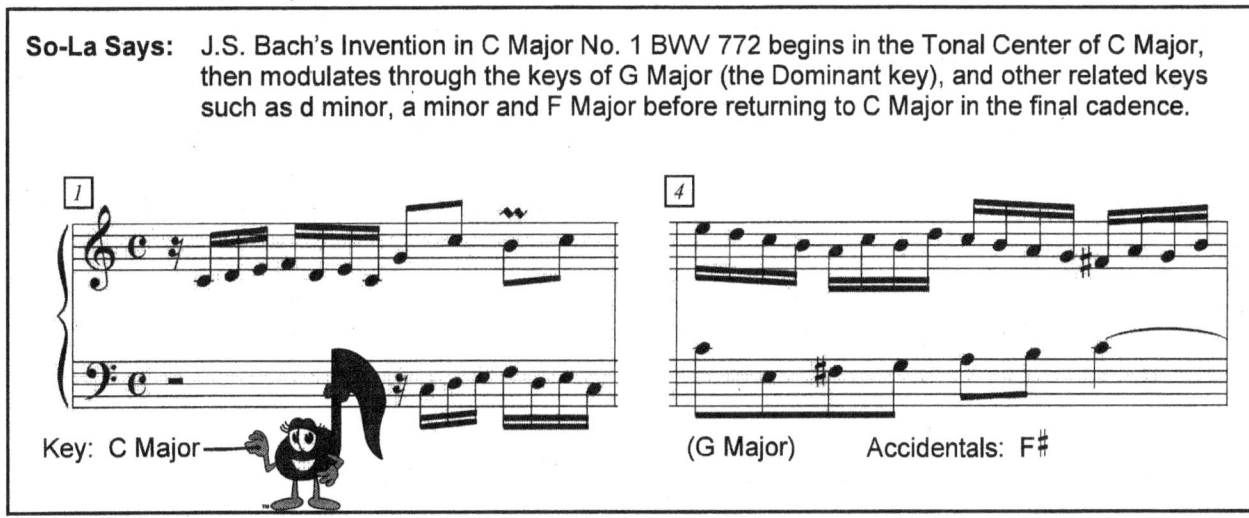

So-La Says: J.S. Bach's Invention in C Major No. 1 BWV 772 begins in the Tonal Center of C Major, then modulates through the keys of G Major (the Dominant key), and other related keys such as d minor, a minor and F Major before returning to C Major in the final cadence.

Key: C Major   (G Major)   Accidentals: F#

♪ **Ti-Do Tip:** Modulation can be indicated by using a new Key Signature or by simply using accidentals to create a new Tonal Center (a new key).

1. The following excerpts are taken from J.S. Bach's Invention in C Major No. 1 BWV 772. Identify the key into which each of these two-measure excerpts is modulating.

a) (Key: __d__ minor)   Accidentals: B♭ C#

b) (Key: __a__ minor)   Accidentals: F# G#

MOTIVE AND SEQUENCE - Use after Intermediate Page 126

A **Motive** is a short pattern that may be repeated as: **Repetition** (same pattern, same voice, same pitch), **Transposition** (same pattern at a different pitch) or **Sequence** (same pattern of two or more consecutive repetitions at a higher or lower pitch).

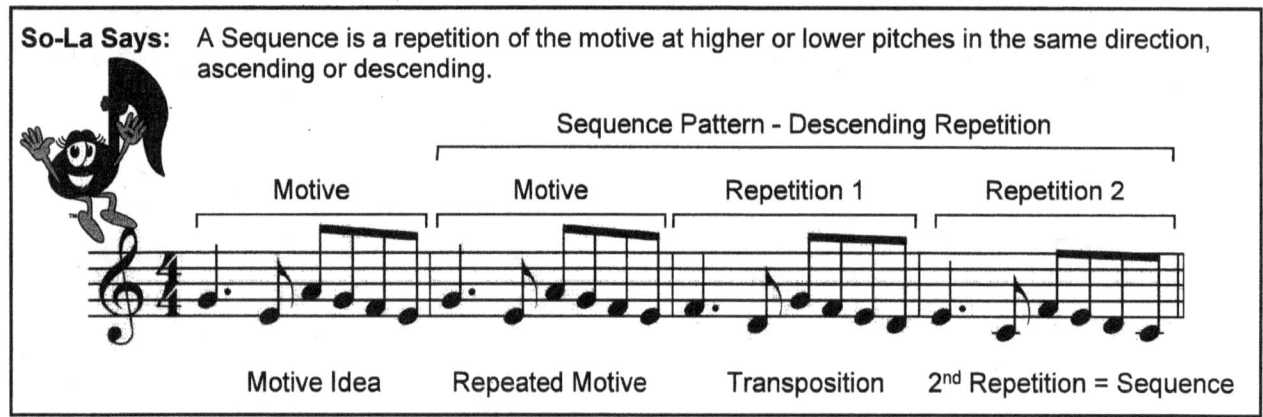

So-La Says: A Sequence is a repetition of the motive at higher or lower pitches in the same direction, ascending or descending.

1. Name the key. Label each of the repeated motive patterns directly above the bracketed measures as: Repetition (same), Transposition (higher or lower) or Sequence (ascending or descending).

   a) Key: **C Major** — *Sequence (descending)*

   b) Key: **G Major** — *Repetition (same)*

   c) Key: **f minor** — *Sequence (ascending)*

   d) Key: **D Major** — *Transposition (lower)*

SEQUENCE - MONOPHONIC, HOMOPHONIC AND POLYPHONIC TEXTURE - Use after Page 126

A **Sequence** in: Monophonic Texture is a melody written as a single voiced melodic line with no accompaniment; Homophonic Texture is a melody written as a single voice with harmonic accompaniment; Polyphonic Texture is a multi-voiced texture that contains two or more equally important melodic lines.

So-La Says: Bach's Invention in C Major is in Polyphonic Texture with two independent melodic lines. Both melodic lines are repeated in a Descending Sequence.

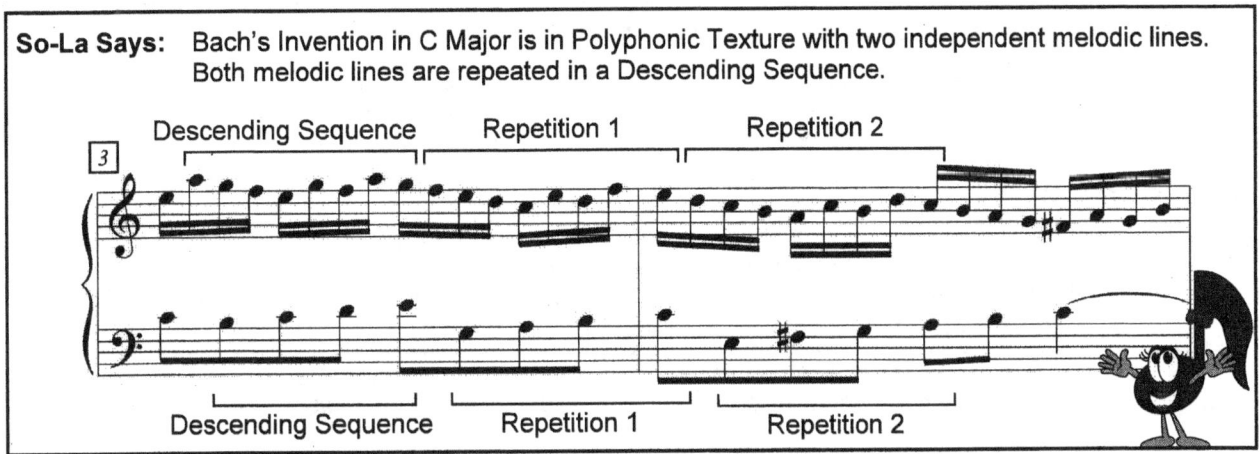

♩ **Ti-Do Tip:** When the rhythm is relatively simple, it is correct to beam together the first two S + w pulses (4 eighth notes) and the last two M + w pulses (4 eighth notes) in "4" time (Common Time).

1. Transpose the Motive from m. 1 into m. 2 and m. 3 to create a Sequence for each of the textures below.

a) Transpose DOWN an interval of a 2nd in each measure to create a Sequence in Monophonic Texture.

b) Transpose UP an interval of a 3rd in each measure to create a Sequence in Homophonic Texture.

c) Transpose DOWN an interval of a 3rd in each measure to create a Sequence in Polyphonic Texture.

MELODY WRITING - MOVEMENTS and ELEMENTS - Use after Intermediate Page 139

Melody Writing requires imagination, practice and knowledge in the types of Melodic Movements and Elements of Music that make melodies interesting, inspiring, exciting, heartfelt, captivating and memorable.

> **So-La Says:** A Melody may be written using three types of Melodic Movements:
>
> **Conjunct** - melody movement by step (ascending or descending);
> **Disjunct** - melody movement by skip or leap (ascending or descending);
> **Stasis** (Greek - standing still) - repetition of a note before movement in a melody.
>
> A Melody has two main Elements of Music:
>
> **Melodic Structure** - the shape (curve) that creates the design (rise and fall) of the melody; (based upon the interval directions - up, down, same).
> **Rhythmic Structure** - the rhythmic pattern that creates the pulse and beat of the melody; (based upon the value of the notes/rests).

1. Identify each of the following Melodic Movements as: Conjunct, Disjunct or Stasis.

a) The melody movement is ___Conjunct___.

b) The melody movement is ___Disjunct___.

c) The melody movement is ___Stasis___.

2. Identify each of the following Elements of Music as: Melodic Structure or Rhythmic Structure.

a) The main element is ___Melodic___ Structure.
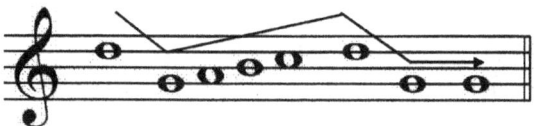

b) The main element is ___Rhythmic___ Structure.

3. Combine the two elements in question 2 a) and 2 b) to form a melody on the staff below.

a) A ___Melody___ combines two main elements, Melodic Structure and Rhythmic Structure.

MELODY WRITING - PARALLEL PERIOD and ANALYSIS - Use after Intermediate Page 139

Melody Writing has structure (Melodic and Rhythmic) and movement (Conjunct, Disjunct or Stasis) that builds a musical phrase. A **Parallel Period**, usually eight measures, contains two four-measure phrases.

The 1st four-measure Phrase "a" (Antecedent or Question) ends on an unstable scale degree (pitch).
The 2nd four-measure Phrase "a1" (Consequent or Answer) ends on a stable scale degree (pitch).

So-La Says: Review the Elements of Melody Writing in the Ultimate Music Theory LEVEL 5 Supplemental Workbook:

Composition of a Parallel Period and Phrase Endings;
Repetition of a Melodic Pattern in Phrase "a" and "a1";
Identification of Stable and Unstable Scale Degrees.

Look at the UMT LEVEL 5 Answer Book to see completed melody writing examples. Use these as a reference.

A Parallel Period has the SAME Melodic Movements and Elements of Music used in mm. 1 - 2 of the first Phrase "a", repeated in mm. 5 - 6 of the second Phrase "a1". The last two measures of each phrase may be similar or different. Phrase "a" ends on an unstable degree ($\hat{2}$, $\hat{7}$), Phrase "a1" ends on a stable degree ($\hat{1}$, $\hat{3}$).

♪ **Ti-Do Tip:** To avoid confusion between a Musical Phrase (slur) and an Analysis Phrase Mark (written over an analyzed section of music), use a Square "⌐⎯⎯⎯⎯⎯¬" Analysis Phrase Mark.

1. Name the key. Copy the movements and elements from mm. 1 - 2 in the first Phrase "a" into mm. 5 - 6 of the second Phrase "a1". Label the final scale degree note in each phrase directly above the staff as: $\hat{1}$, $\hat{2}$, $\hat{3}$ or $\hat{7}$. Draw an Analysis Phrase Mark over mm. 5 - 8 and label it as: "a1".

Key: __A Major__

2. Analyze the music by answering the questions below. Sing or Play the Parallel Period melody.

   a) Circle if the melodic movement in mm. 1 - 2 and 5 - 6 is: Conjunct   or   (Disjunct)   or   Stasis.

   b) Identify the following for the chord in measure 1: Root: __A__   Type/Quality: __Major__

   c) Identify the following for the chord in measure 2: Root: __E__   Type/Quality: __Dominant 7th__

   d) Circle if the melodic structure in mm. 3 - 4 and 7 - 8 is: same   or   similar   or   (different.)

   e) Circle if the cadence ending Phrase "a" is: Authentic Cadence (Perfect) or (Half Cadence (Imperfect).)

   f) Circle if the cadence ending Phrase "a1" is: (Authentic Cadence (Perfect)) or Half Cadence (Imperfect).

MELODY WRITING - PARALLEL PERIOD - CADENCE VOICE LEADING - Use after Page 139

In a Parallel Period, each four-measure Phrase "a" and "a1" ends the Chord Progression with a **Cadence**. When writing a Parallel Period (monophonic texture), the cadence is not written out in full. It is "implied".

The first Question Phrase "a" ends with a **Half Cadence** (I - V, i - V or IV - V, iv - V) on an unstable scale degree ($\hat{5}$, $\hat{7}$, $\hat{2}$ of the Dominant triad).

The second Answer Phrase "a1" ends with an **Authentic Cadence** (V - I or V - i) on a stable scale degree ($\hat{1}$, $\hat{3}$, $\hat{5}$ or the Upper Tonic $\hat{8}(\hat{1})$ of the Tonic triad).

The Dominant ($\hat{5}$) is both a stable and unstable scale degree. It is the **Common Note** between the Tonic and Dominant chords. In the Tonic chord, the Tonic ($\hat{1}$) can be used as either $\hat{1}$ or $\hat{8}(\hat{1})$ - Upper Tonic.

So-La Says: "Voice Leading" means the gradual movement of notes between chords in a progression. Voice Leading (vocal or instrumental) is based upon the melodies of vocal music.

Tonic Chord I or i	Subdominant Chord IV or iv	Dominant Chord V
$\hat{1}(\hat{8})$, $\hat{3}$, $\hat{5}$	$\hat{4}$, $\hat{6}$, $\hat{1}(\hat{8})$	$\hat{5}$, $\hat{7}$, $\hat{2}$

The best Voice Leading between chords is: **Stasis**, **Conjunct** or **Disjunct** (skip).

Cadence Voice Leading Chart: **C Major**
- V: $\hat{5}$ - **G** $\hat{7}$ - **B** $\hat{2}$ - **D**
- IV: $\hat{4}$ - **F** $\hat{6}$ - **A** $\hat{1}(\hat{8})$ - **C**
- I: $\hat{1}(\hat{8})$ - **C** $\hat{3}$ - **E** $\hat{5}$ - **G**

♫ **Ti-Do Tip:** Cadence Triad Scale Degree notes are used as the melody notes. The performer can play the chords "implied" by the notes to create a homophonic or polyphonic accompaniment.

Stasis Voice Leading (movement by repetition):

Half Cadence (i - V, I - V): $\hat{5}\rightarrow\hat{5}$.

Half Cadence (IV - V, iv - V): No Common Note

Authentic Cadence (V - I, V - i): $\hat{5}\rightarrow\hat{5}$.

1. Add the missing notes to complete each Cadence using Stasis Voice Leading.

Half Cadence   Authentic Cadence

Conjunct Voice Leading (movement by step):

Half Cadence (i - V, I - V): Step down = $\hat{3}\rightarrow\hat{2}$; $\hat{8}\rightarrow\hat{7}$; Step up = $\hat{1}\rightarrow\hat{2}$.

Half Cadence (IV - V, iv - V): Step down = $\hat{6}\rightarrow\hat{5}$; $\hat{8}\rightarrow\hat{7}$.

Authentic Cadence (V - I, V - i): Step down = $\hat{2}\rightarrow\hat{1}$; Step up = $\hat{7}\rightarrow\hat{8}$; $\hat{2}\rightarrow\hat{3}$.

2. Add the missing notes to complete each Cadence using Conjunct Voice Leading.

Half Cadence   Authentic Cadence

Disjunct Voice Leading (movement by skip):

Half Cadence (i - V, I - V): Skip up = $\hat{3}\nearrow\hat{5}$; $\hat{5}\nearrow\hat{7}$.

Half Cadence (IV - V, iv - V): Skip down = $\hat{4}\searrow\hat{2}$.

Authentic Cadence (V - I, V - i): Skip down = $\hat{5}\searrow\hat{3}$.

(*Preferable to not use $\hat{7}\searrow\hat{5}$ as the final melody line.)

3. Add the missing notes to complete each Cadence using Disjunct Voice Leading.

Half Cadence   Authentic Cadence

MELODY WRITING - PARALLEL PERIOD - HARMONIC PROGRESSION - Use after Page 139

A **Harmonic Progression** or **Chord Progression** is the foundation of harmony that establishes the tonality or "key" of the piece and supports the melody. Chord Progressions may be indicated by Roman Numerals.

Functional Chord Symbols (Roman Numerals) written below the staff indicate the Harmonic Progression. The SAME Harmonic Progression (I, IV, I, V, I, etc.) may be used with DIFFERENT Melodic Phrases.

So-La Says: A Disjunct Melody may outline the notes of a Chord. A Conjunct Melody may include non-triad notes or Passing Tones (pt) that connect triad tones with stepwise motion.

A Parallel Period of two four-measure Phrases, "a" and "a1", will use the SAME Melody and Harmonic Progression in the first two measures of each phrase. The last two measures of each phrase are different.

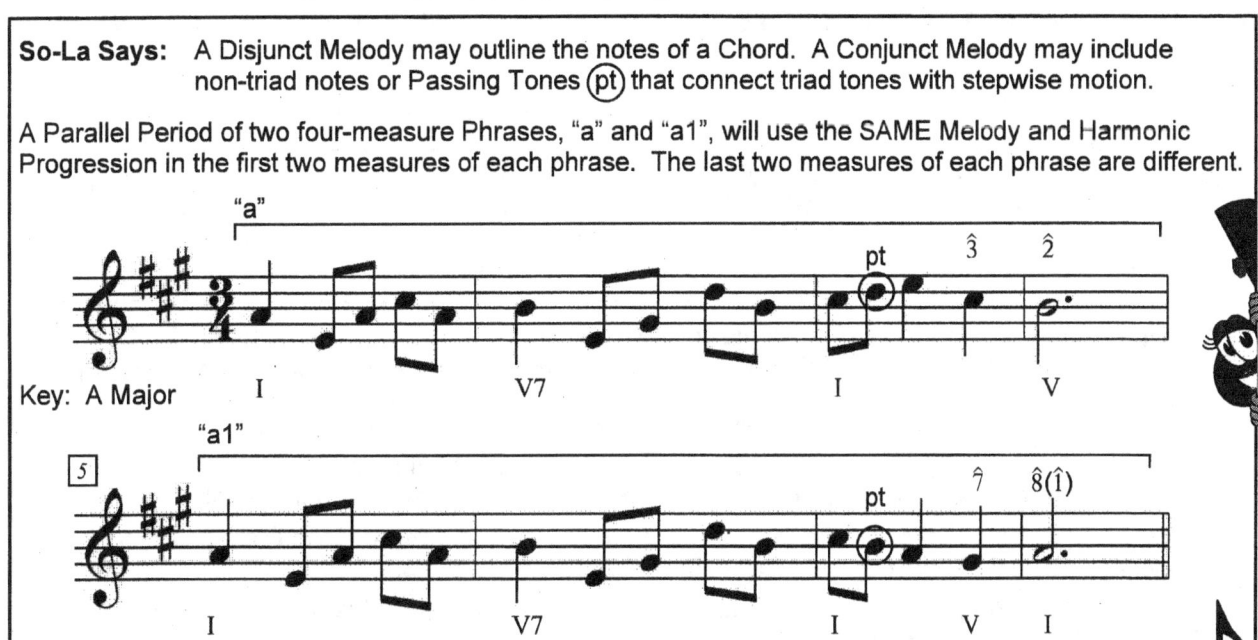

♪ Ti-Do Tip: A strong final ending for a melody is on the Tonic, stable scale degree $\hat{1}$. Step into the Tonic ($\hat{7}$ - $\hat{8}$ ($\hat{1}$) or $\hat{2}$ - $\hat{1}$) on the first beat of the final measure ending on $\hat{1}$. An Authentic Cadence (V - I) usually ends on the Tonic ($\hat{1}$), on Strong Beat 1.

1. Different Melodies in different keys may use the SAME Harmonic Progression. Use the same Harmonic Progression as in the Example above to complete the following for the Parallel Period (Question and Answer Phrases) below. Name the key.

   a) Observing the Harmonic Progression (Functional Chord Symbols), complete the first phrase, ending on an unstable scale degree. Label the scale degree directly above the last note of the phrase.

   b) Compose an answer phrase for the Parallel Period ending on a stable scale degree (preferably the Tonic) to indicate an Authentic Cadence. Label the scale degree above the last note of the phrase.

   c) Draw a square Analysis Phrase Mark over each phrase and label them as "a" or "a1". *(one possible answer)*

Key: **G Major**

PARALLEL PERIOD - FUNCTIONAL and ROOT QUALITY CHORD SYMBOLS - Use after Page 139

When Sight Reading a piece or writing a melody, there are 2 ways to identify **Chord Progression Symbols**:
Functional Chord Symbols - written below the melody identifying the Harmonic Progression;
Root/Quality Chord Symbols - written above the melody to specifically identify the chord name.

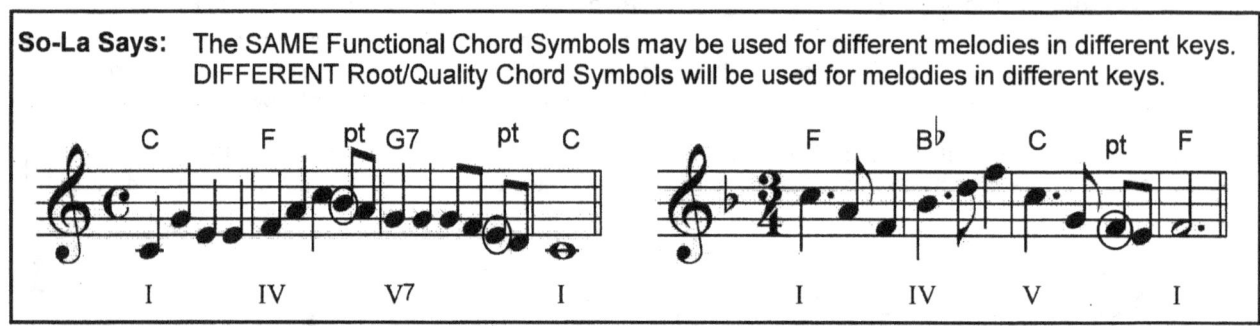

So-La Says: The SAME Functional Chord Symbols may be used for different melodies in different keys. DIFFERENT Root/Quality Chord Symbols will be used for melodies in different keys.

♫ **Ti-Do Tip:** When transposing a piece of music, the Functional Chord Symbols will remain the SAME. The Root/Quality Chord Symbols will be DIFFERENT (to reflect the notes of the new key).

1. Complete the following for each of the Parallel Period melodies below. Name the key.

   a) Observing the Chord Symbols, complete the Antecedent or Question phrase ending on an unstable scale degree. Label the scale degree directly above the last note of the phrase.

   b) Compose a Consequent or Answer phrase. End on a stable scale degree to indicate an Authentic Cadence. Label the scale degree directly above the last note of the phrase.

   c) Write the Chord Progression Symbols both above and below the staff in the answer phrase.

MELODY WRITING - PARALLEL PERIOD - TIPS & TRICKS - Use after Page 139

A Parallel Period Melody must repeat Measures 1 and 2 (melody, rhythm, Functional Chord Symbols and Root Quality Chord Symbols) in Measures 5 and 6. Simply COPY those measures.

> **So-La Says:** One little "trick" that works every time, when completing Phrase "a" in a parallel period, is to end on an unstable degree $\hat{5}$, $\hat{7}$ or $\hat{2}$. When completing Phrase "a1", end on the Tonic, $\hat{1}$.

♫ **Ti-Do Tip:** When writing a melody, use the KISS method. **K**eep **I**t **S**uper **S**imple!

Plan ahead. Identify your Cadences and write your Cadence Voice Leading notes first to establish where the melody will end. A melody may move by step (Conjunct) up or down or move by skip (Disjunct - outlining the chord) or use repeated notes (Stasis).

Use Chord Notes to write your melody. Add Passing Tones to connect intervals of a 3rd.

Sing or play your melody on your instrument. Listen to the melodic line.

1. Complete the Parallel Period melodies below. Name the key.
    a) Complete the first phrase ending on an unstable scale degree. Label the scale degree directly above the last note of the phrase.
    b) Compose an answer phrase to create a parallel period, ending on a stable scale degree. Label the scale degree directly above the last note of the phrase.
    c) Write the Chord Progression Symbols both above and below the staff in the answer phrase.
    d) Draw a square Analysis Phrase Mark over each phrase (below the Chord Symbols) and label them as "a" or "a1". *(one possible answer)*

BUILDING BLOCKS OF BINARY FORM - Use after Page 144

Form in Music is the shape or musical design used as building blocks to create the structure of a piece; just as an architect prepares a blueprint design used as building blocks to create the structure of a building. There are many different forms in music, just as there are many different design forms of buildings.

One Form is called **Binary Form**, a specific design including a motive, phrase pairs (period) and cadences.

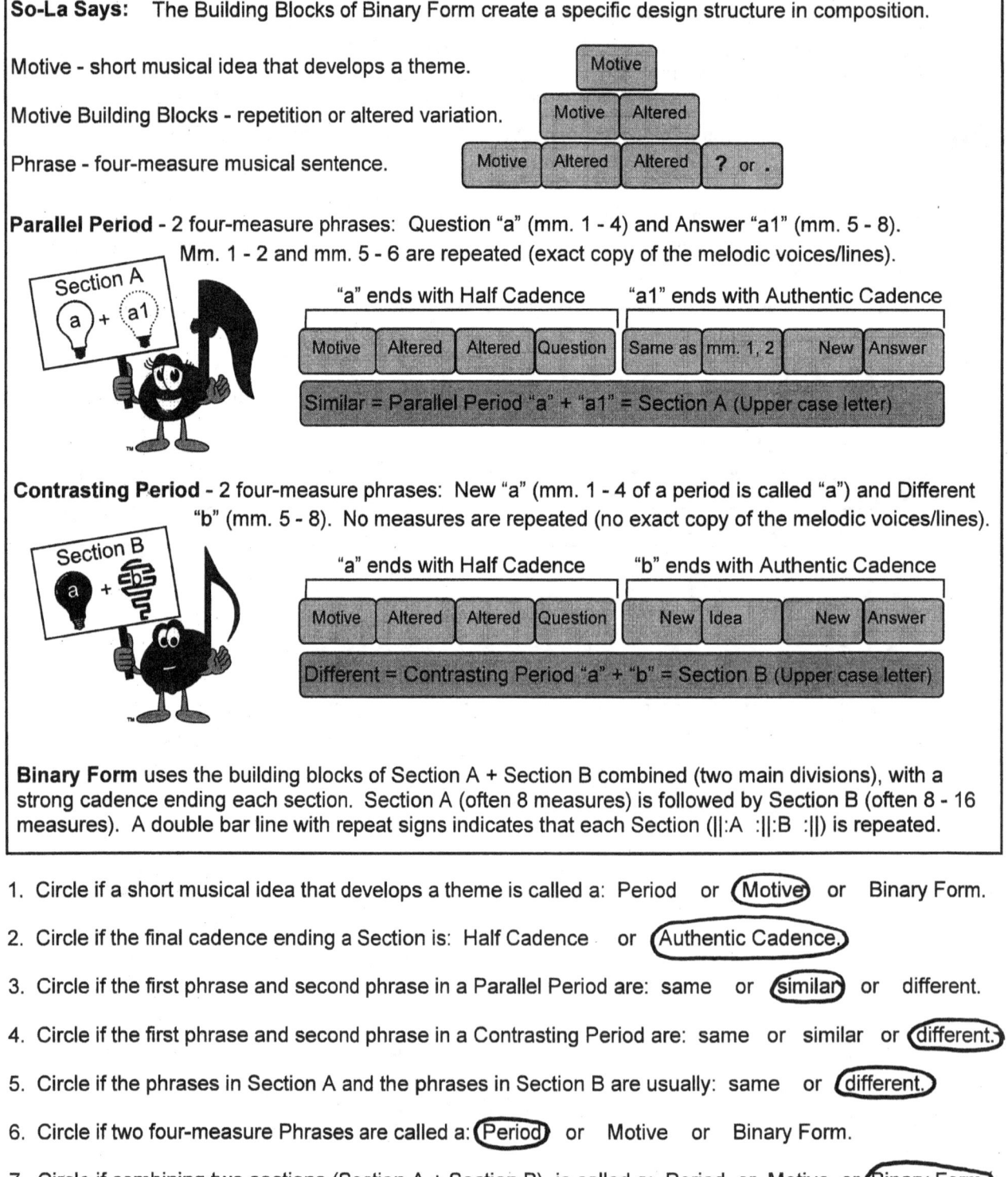

1. Circle if a short musical idea that develops a theme is called a: Period or (Motive) or Binary Form.

2. Circle if the final cadence ending a Section is: Half Cadence or (Authentic Cadence).

3. Circle if the first phrase and second phrase in a Parallel Period are: same or (similar) or different.

4. Circle if the first phrase and second phrase in a Contrasting Period are: same or similar or (different).

5. Circle if the phrases in Section A and the phrases in Section B are usually: same or (different).

6. Circle if two four-measure Phrases are called a: (Period) or Motive or Binary Form.

7. Circle if combining two sections (Section A + Section B), is called a: Period or Motive or (Binary Form).

FORM and ANALYSIS - BINARY FORM

Binary Form is identified by two main Sections, Parallel Period A and Contrasting Period B (Upper case letters), often written above the staff. Phrases within a Period may be identified as: "a", "a1" or "b" (lower case letters), written above the phrase mark or square bracket indicating same, similar or different material.

When the melody line (Voice Leading) in a (V - I , V7 - I) Cadence ends on $\hat{1}$ (or $\hat{8}$) in the Soprano, and the Dominant and Tonic notes are in the Bass Voice, it is a strong Perfect Authentic Cadence (PAC) ending.

So-La Says: A cadence may begin on a strong beat or a weak beat in one measure, and end on the strong beat (beat 1) in the next measure. The Dominant triad may use V or V7.

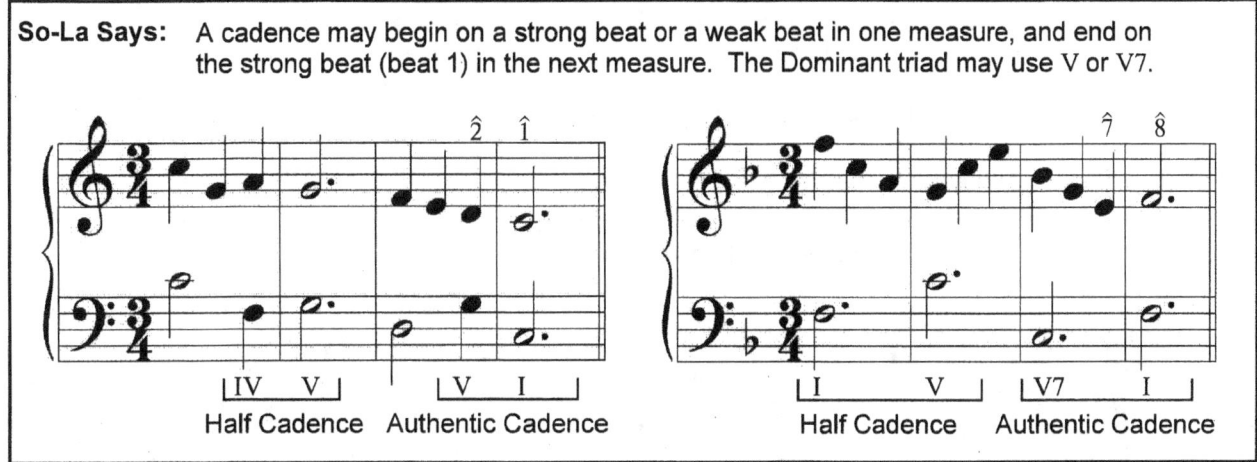

♪ **Ti-Do Tip:** Half Cadence (I - V; IV - V): Dominant, scale degree $\hat{5}$, in Bass; unfinished, a "question".
Authentic Cadence (V - I; V7 - I): Tonic, scale degree $\hat{1}$, in Bass; finished, a "period".

1. Analyze the music by answering the questions below. Name the key. Play (Sight Read) the piece.

Key: **G Major**

a) Name the type of Period (2 four-measure phrases) indicated at the letter A. **Parallel Period**

b) Name the type of Period (2 four-measure phrases) indicated at the letter B. **Contrasting Period**

c) Label each of the 4 phrase groups directly above each square bracket as: "a" or "a1" or "b".

d) Label each of the 4 cadences directly below the staff in the square bracket as: I - V or IV - V or V - I.

e) The form structure of this composition (Section A + Section B) is called **Binary Form**.

FORM and ANALYSIS - BINARY FORM - SIMPLE, BALANCED and BARFORM

Binary Form: "Bi" = 2. Binary Form is a 2 Section Structural Form of a movement or piece (often repeated). The two sections are identified as: Section A (first section), Section A' (similar to A) or Section B (different).

> **So-La Says:** There are several different types of Binary (Two Section) Form.
>
> **Simple Binary**: Two sections may be: **similar** A and A' (||:A :||:A' :||) or **different** A and B (||:A :||:B :||). In Simple Binary, **both** sections end with a PAC, a Perfect Authentic Cadence (ending on the Tonic).
>
> **Balanced Binary**: Second half of Section A ("*") returns as the second half of Section B (||:A *:||:B *:||).
>
> **Barform**: Section A is repeated, Section B is not repeated (||:A :||B ||). Both sections end with a PAC.

1. Complete the Binary Form Chart below as: Simple Binary, Balanced Binary or Barform.

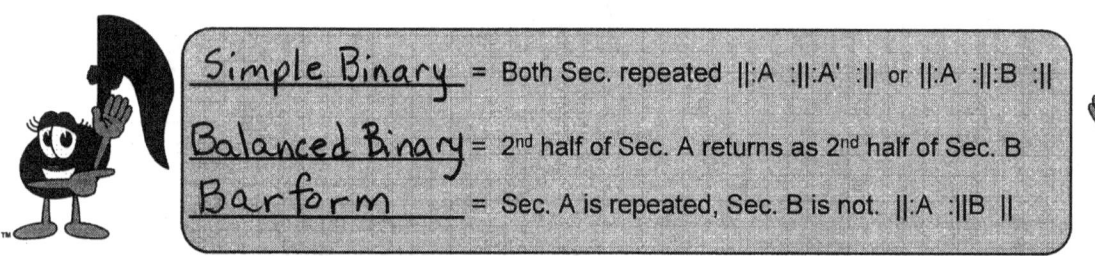

__Simple Binary__ = Both Sec. repeated ||:A :||:A' :|| or ||:A :||:B :||
__Balanced Binary__ = 2nd half of Sec. A returns as 2nd half of Sec. B
__Barform__ = Sec. A is repeated, Sec. B is not. ||:A :||B ||

2. Analyze the music by answering the questions below. Name the key. Play (Sight Read) the piece.

Key: __F Major__

a) Name the type of Period (two four-measure phrases) indicated at the letter A. __Parallel Period__

b) Name the type of Period (two four-measure phrases) indicated at the letter B. __Contrasting Period__

c) Circle if the four-measure phrase in mm. 5 - 8 and in mm. 13 - 16 are: (same) or different.

d) Label each of the 4 cadences directly below the staff in the square bracket as: I - V or IV - V or V - I.

e) The Binary Form structure of this piece is called __Balanced__ Binary.

FORM and ANALYSIS - STRUCTURAL FORM - ROUNDED BINARY and TERNARY FORM

Structural Form and balancing phrases and sections were an important part of Classical Music. The most popular **Structural Forms** were **Simple Binary Form** (two sections) and **Ternary Form** (three sections).

Rounded Binary: "Round" in music refers to "coming back around" to the same material. Material from Section A or A' returns in Section B as: ABA (||:A :||:BA :||) or as ABA' (||:A :||:BA' :||).

Ternary Form: The third section is the same or similar to the first, ABA or ABA' (with or without repeats). To save space, Composers would often use a DC al Fine at the end of Section B (to repeat Section A).

Rounded Binary	**Section A**	**Section B or A'**	**(Rounding)**
||:A I	→ Modulate to V → Half Cadence (HC) on V → PAC on I	:||:B Phrase B or A' In the Key of V or on V	Return of A Modulate to I PAC on I :||

Ternary Form	**Section A**	**Section B**	**Section A**
||:A	PAC on I	:||:B B or varied A Motion to new key Cadence PAC or HC	:||:A Phrase A or A' end on I :||

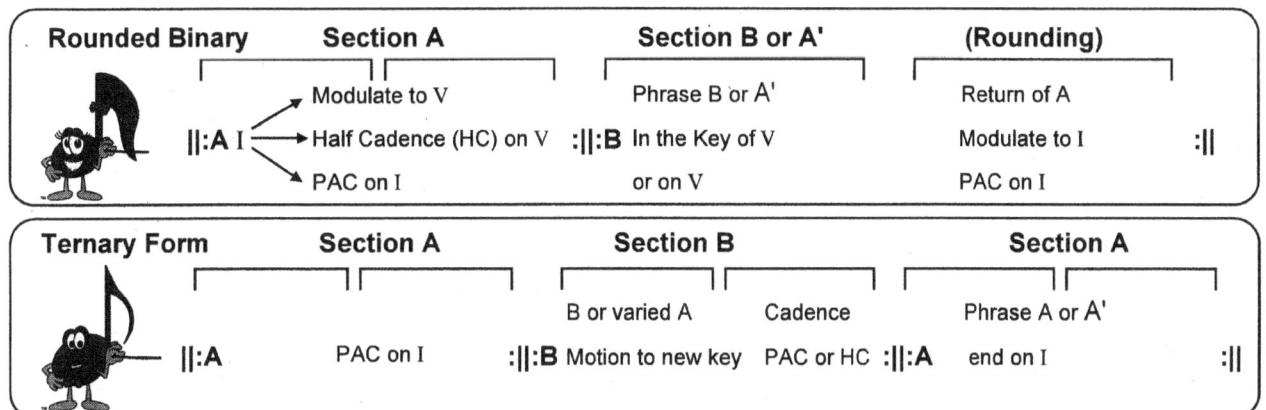

♫ **Ti-Do Tip:** In a Perfect Authentic Cadence (PAC) the V - I chords are in root position (the root of each chord is in the Bass voice). The Tonic note will be in the top voice of Chord I.

1. Analyze the music by answering the questions below. Name the key. Play (Sight Read) the piece.

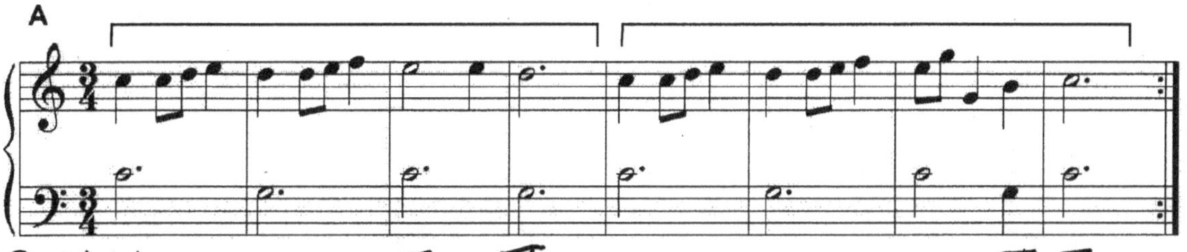

A

Key: C Major [I V] [V I]

B

[I V] [V I]

a) Name the type of Period (two four-measure phrases) indicated at the letter A. Parallel Period

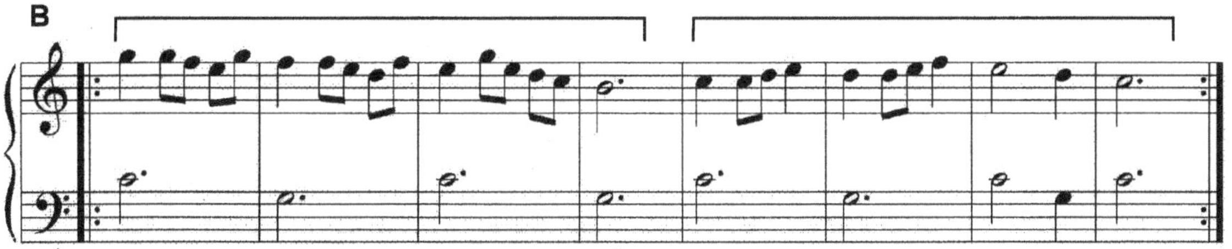

b) Name the type of Period (two four-measure phrases) indicated at the letter B. Contrasting Period

c) Circle if the four-measure phrase in mm. 1 - 4 and mm. 13 - 16 are: (similar) or different.

d) Label each of the 4 cadences directly below the staff in the square bracket as: I - V or IV - V or V - I.

e) The Binary Form structure of this piece is called Rounded Binary.

IMAGINE, COMPOSE, EXPLORE

♪ **I**magine - Use your imagination to create a title that describes your composition.
♪ **C**ompose - Write your composition and add your name (top right) as the composer.
♪ **E**xplore - Add "So-La Sparkles" (terms & signs) to express how the music is played.

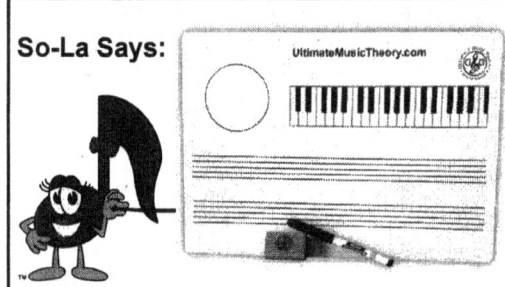

So-La Says:

When composing follow these 3 Composing Steps:

1. Record your melody as you play. Use it as a reference.
2. Write your melody on the Whiteboard. Try different ideas.
3. Write your melody in the workbook. Add "So-La Sparkles" of articulation, dynamics, etc. to create your final composition.

1. Complete the following melody to create a Parallel Period. Add a title and your name as the composer.

    a) Name the key. Add the correct Time Signature directly below the bracket.
    b) Complete the first Question phrase ending on an unstable scale degree. Label the degree number.
    c) Compose the Answer phrase ending on a stable scale degree. Label the degree number.
    d) Add functional chord symbols below each measure as needed. Add "So-La Sparkles" etc. and Play!

My Best **Friend So-La**
(title)

Ti-Do + Friends
(composer)

Key: **G Major**

♫ **Ti-Do Time:** Get your "Composers Certificate". SCAN your composition (on this page) and send it to us at: info@ultimatemusictheory.com and we will send you a special **Ultimate Music Theory Composers Certificate** - FREE.

ANALYSIS and SIGHT READING

1. Analyze the music by answering the questions below. Play (Sight Read) the piece "The Lizard".

   a) Add the correct Time Signature directly below the bracket.

   b) At letter A, circle if the melodic line in the R.H. and the L.H. is the: (same,) similar or different.

   c) Name the interval at letter B. __min 3__ Name both notes, lower note first. __F#__ __A__

   d) Name the notes at letter C. __F__ __F#__ __F♮__ Circle if the half steps are: (chromatic) or diatonic.

   e) At letter D, explain the Dynamic: for the R.H.: __p soft__; for the L.H.: __f loud__.

   f) Identify the scale at letter E. __octatonic__ Identify the number of notes in the scale. __9__

   g) For the chord at letter F, identify the following: Note Names, lowest note first: __E♭__ __G__ __C__
   Root: __C__ Type/Quality: __minor__ Root/Quality Chord Symbol: __Cm/E♭__

   h) For the chord at letter G, identify the following: Note Names, lowest note first: __E__ __G__ __C__
   Root: __C__ Type/Quality: __Major__ Root/Quality Chord Symbol: __C/E__

MUSIC HISTORY - BAROQUE ERA (1600 - 1750) AND BACH

The term Baroque (Portuguese - *barroco*, Italian - *barocco*) means a pearl of irregular shape, like the jewelry of the time. Baroque art and music are divided into three 50 year periods: early, middle and late Baroque.

Baroque Era - Composer	Genre	Work
Early Baroque (1600 - 1650)		
Claudio Monteverdi (1567 - 1643)	Opera	Orfeo and The Coronation of Poppea
Middle Baroque (1650 - 1700)		
Henry Purcell (1659 - 1695)	Opera	Dido and Aeneas
Late Baroque (1700 - 1750)		
Antonio Vivaldi (1678 - 1741)	Concerto	Violin Concerto - The Four Seasons
Johann Sebastian Bach (1685 - 1750)	Solo Keyboard	Invention in C Major No. 1 BWV 772

Music Historians consider the Baroque Period to have ended with the death of J.S. Bach. Bach took String Concertos from Italian masters, such as Vivaldi, and arranged them for solo harpsichord. He added ornaments and new inner voices (contrapuntal texture) to these **Secular** (non-religious) works.

J. S. Bach's devout Lutheran faith is evident in his hundreds of **Sacred** (religious) works (Cantatas, Oratorios, Passions) written for church services to express a love of God.

"The aim and final reason of all music should be nothing else but the Glory of God and the refreshment of the spirit." ~ Johann Sebastian Bach

In the UMT LEVEL 3 Supplemental Workbook, you learned about the music of J.S. Bach, Baroque Dances and the Notebook for Anna Magdalena written for Solo Keyboard (usually performed on a harpsichord).

In 1723, Bach, a harpsichord virtuoso, published a Secular series of Two-Part Inventions in 15 keys: C Maj, c min, D Maj, d min, E flat Maj, E Maj, e min, F Maj, f min, G Maj, g min, A Maj, a min, B flat Maj and b min.

A **Two-Part Invention** is a contrapuntal piece written for 2 Voices/Parts. The melody of each voice/part is equally important. Polyphonic Texture (multi-voiced texture) is created when both melodic lines are played together. Performing Forces: solo keyboard instrument (harpsichord, clavichord).

Today, Bach's Two-Part Inventions may be played on the piano (solo keyboard instrument) or played by two instruments (eg. violin & cello), with each instrument playing one voice part creating the polyphonic texture.

Go to **GSGMUSIC.com** - For Easy Access to listening to Bach Invention in C Major No. 1 BWV 772 played on various Performing Forces including the harpsichord, clavichord, piano and duet for violin and cello.

1. Name the Baroque period of J.S. Bach as: early, middle or late Baroque. __Late Baroque__

2. J.S. Bach wrote Sacred (religious) works and __Secular__ (non-religious) works.

3. In 1723 Bach published his Secular work of Two-Part Inventions in __15__ different Major and minor keys.

4. A Two-Part Invention is a __contrapuntal__ piece written for __2__ Voices/Parts.

5. Two melodic lines combined into a multi-voiced texture is called __polyphonic__ texture.

6. The Genre of Bach's Two-Part Invention in C Major is called __Solo Keyboard__.

7. Bach's Inventions were written for the Performing Forces of __harpsichord (solo keyboard) (clavichord)__

MUSIC HISTORY - J.S. BACH - INVENTION IN C MAJOR NO. 1 BWV 772

J.S. Bach's Two-Part Inventions are in contrapuntal texture or counterpoint (Latin *contra punctum* meaning "point against point"). This "melody against melody" relationship has two voices, each with an independent melody. These harmonically interdependent melodies create polyphonic texture when played together.

Bach's Invention in C Major has an 8 Note Motive that is developed using various contrapuntal devices.

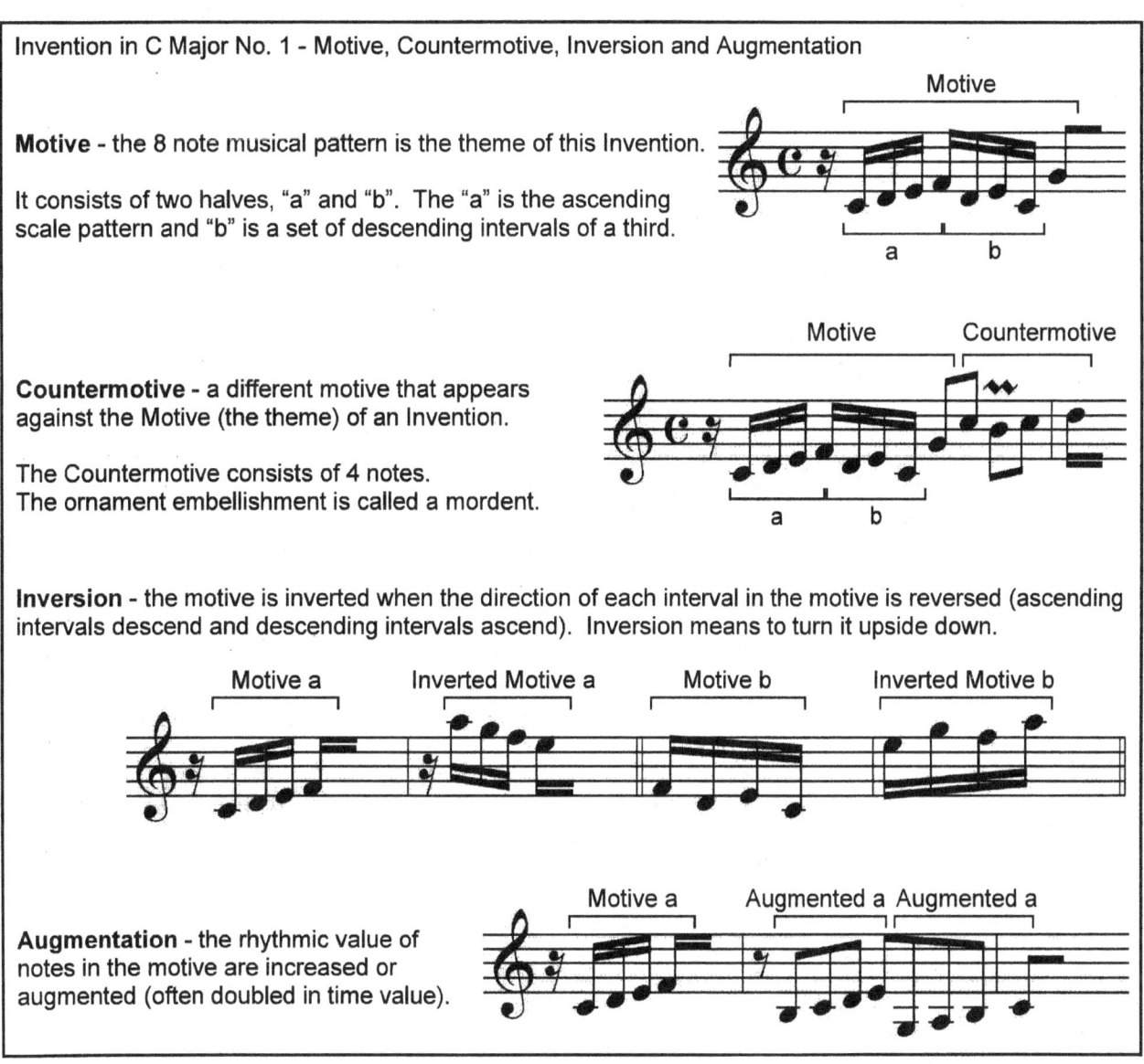

Go to **GSGMUSIC.com** - For Easy Access to watch videos on the performance of the Invention in C Major.

1. The 8 note musical pattern in the first measure of Bach's Invention in C Major is called the _Motive_
2. A different musical pattern also developed in this Invention is called the _Counter Motive_.
3. When a motive is inverted and the direction is reversed it is called an _inversion_.
4. When the rhythmic time value of notes in the motive are increased it is called _augmentation_.
5. The Invention in C Major No. 1 BWV 772 was written by _J.S. Bach_

MUSIC HISTORY - J.S. BACH - INVENTION IN C MAJOR NO. 1 BWV 772 - ANALYSIS SECTION 1

Two-Part Invention in C Major No. 1 - Part 1 is played with the RH and Part 2 is played with the LH. The Invention is divided into three sections: Section I mm. 1 - 7; Section II mm. 7 - 15; Section III mm. 15 - 22.

> **Imitation** - immediate repetition of the motive in a second voice/part (same or different pitch).
> **Transposition** - repetition of the motive at a different pitch, in the same voice (same or different clef).
> **Sequence** - 2 or more consecutive repetitions of the motive at a higher or lower pitch in the same voice.

1. Analyze Bach's Two-Part Invention in C Major No. 1, Section I mm. 1 - 7, by filling in the blanks below.

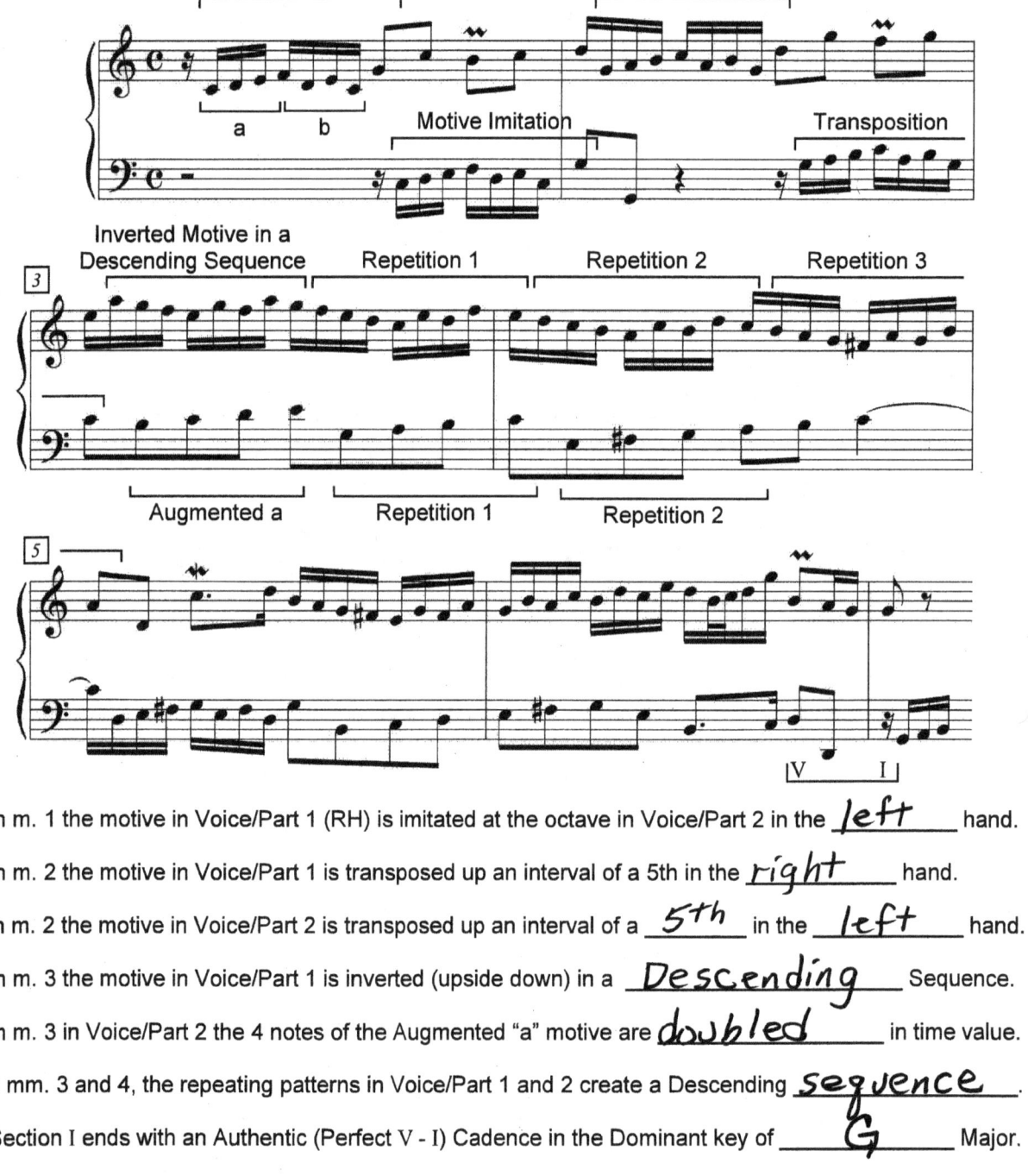

a) In m. 1 the motive in Voice/Part 1 (RH) is imitated at the octave in Voice/Part 2 in the __left__ hand.

b) In m. 2 the motive in Voice/Part 1 is transposed up an interval of a 5th in the __right__ hand.

c) In m. 2 the motive in Voice/Part 2 is transposed up an interval of a __5th__ in the __left__ hand.

d) In m. 3 the motive in Voice/Part 1 is inverted (upside down) in a __Descending__ Sequence.

e) In m. 3 in Voice/Part 2 the 4 notes of the Augmented "a" motive are __doubled__ in time value.

f) In mm. 3 and 4, the repeating patterns in Voice/Part 1 and 2 create a Descending __sequence__.

g) Section I ends with an Authentic (Perfect V - I) Cadence in the Dominant key of __G__ Major.

MUSIC HISTORY - J.S. BACH - INVENTION IN C MAJOR NO. 1 BWV 772 - ANALYSIS SECTION 2

Two-Part Invention in C Major No. 1 illustrates the use of contrapuntal devices: Inversion, Augmentation, Imitation, Transposition and Sequence in Sec. I mm. 1 - 7, Sec. II mm. 7 - 15 and Sec. III mm. 15 - 22.

> **Double Counterpoint** (Invertible Counterpoint) - a polyphonic passage, written for two voices so that the melodies of the two voices can be switched between the upper and lower voices with acceptable results.

1. Analyze Bach's Two-Part Invention in C Major No. 1, Section II mm. 7 - 15, by filling in the blanks below.

a) In m. 7 the motive in Voice/Part 2 followed by Voice/Part 1 are now in the Dominant key of __G__ Major.

b) The voice inversion (switched voices) between mm. 1 - 2 and mm. 7 - 8 is __Double__ Counterpoint.
   , (invertible)

c) In mm. 9 in Voice/Part 2 followed by Voice/Part 1, the motive is __inverted__.

d) In m. 12 in Voice/Part 1 the motive "a" is Augmented; the time value of the notes are __doubled__.

e) In m. 13 the Motive is played in Voice/Part __1__ in the __right__ hand.

f) In m 14. the Inverted Motive "b" is written twice in Voice/Part __2__ in the __left__ hand.

g) Section II ends with an Authentic (Perfect V - i) Cadence in the relative minor key of __a__ minor.

MUSIC HISTORY - J.S. BACH - INVENTION IN C MAJOR NO. 1 BWV 772 - ANALYSIS SECTION 3

Two-Part Invention in C Major No. 1 is organized in three sections, each one demonstrating different handling of contrapuntal devices. Section I mm. 1 - 7, Section II mm. 7 - 15, Section III mm. 15 - 22.

> The 8 note motive of Bach's Invention in C Major uses contrapuntal devices of Inversion, Augmentation, Imitation, Transposition and Sequence to create a polyphonic texture with imitative counterpoint.

1. Analyze Bach's Two-Part Invention in C Major No. 1, Section III mm. 15 - 22, by answering the questions.

a) In m. 15 label the Voice/Part 1 directly above the bracket as: Motive Inversion or Motive Augmentation.

b) In m. 16 label the Voice/Part 2 directly below the bracket as: Motive Augmentation or Motive Imitation.

e) In m. 18 label the Voice/Part 1 directly above the bracket as: Motive or Motive Inversion or Augmented.

c) In m. 19 label the inverted Voice/Part 2 directly below the bracket as: Augmented "a" or Augmented "b".

d) In mm. 19 - 20 the repeated pattern in both Voice Parts at a higher pitch is called a _Sequence_.

f) Section III ends with an _Authentic_ Cadence (V^7 - I) in the Tonic key of _C_ Major.

g) 3 Contrapuntal devices used in this piece are: _inversion_, _imitation_, _augmentation_

J.S. BACH - INVENTION IN C MAJOR NO. 1 BWV 772 - ANALYSIS REVIEW & COMPOSITION

Bach's 15 Inventions not only provide exercises for both hands but also for every finger. The contrapuntal devices used create the distinct characteristics to build a complete work that evolves from a simple motive.

> A melody begins with a motive (short rhythmic and/or melodic idea) that forms a shape or contour that is recognizable, memorable and repeated using various contrapuntal devices. A motive provides unity and logic as it weaves a relationship into the polyphonic texture of the musical fabric.

1. Analyze the contrapuntal devices used in the Invention in C Major by answering the questions below.

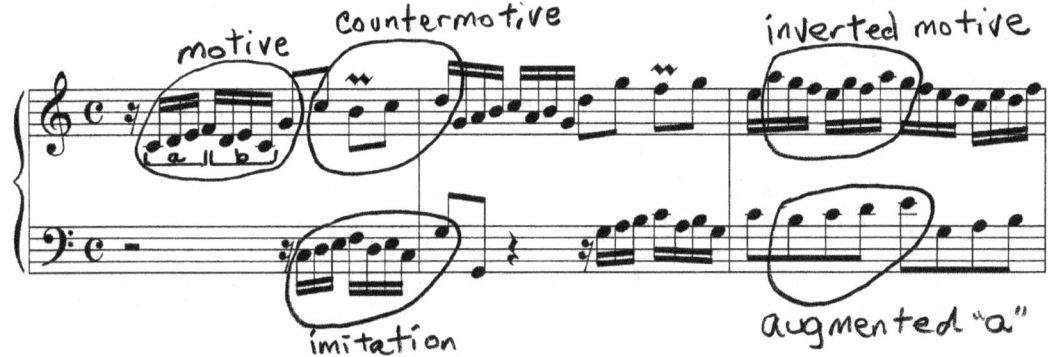

a) Circle and label the Motive directly on the music. Label part "a" and "b". The motive has __8__ notes.

b) Circle and label the Countermotive directly on the music. The countermotive has __4__ notes.

c) The ornament embellishment in the Countermotive is called a __mordent__.

d) Circle and label an example of Imitation of the motive directly on the music.

e) Circle and label an example of Inversion of the motive directly on the music.

f) Circle and label an example of Augmentation "a" of the motive part "a" directly on the music.

> The Baroque Period is 1600 - 1750. Bach's Invention in C Major No. 1 is in the Genre of Solo Keyboard. The 21st Century Period is 2000 - today. Inventions composed today are in the Genre of Solo Keyboard.

2. Transpose the melody in m. 1 down one octave into the Bass Clef. Observe the half rest. Start on beat 3. Transpose the melody in m. 1 up an interval of a fifth into measure 2 in the Treble Clef. Start on beat 1. Use your UMT Ruler to line up stems correctly.

Go to **GSGMUSIC.com** - For Easy Access to watch videos on various Solo Keyboard instruments.

MUSIC HISTORY - J.S. BACH - BRANDENBURG CONCERTOS

Bach wrote in the Genre of Solo Keyboard and in the Genre of Concerto (*concerto* means concert). There are two types of concertos: **solo concerto** - solo instrument and accompanying instrumental group, and **concerto grosso** (*concerti grossi*) - more than one soloist (2 - 4) and accompanying instrumental group.

Bach's six *concerti grossi* - Brandenburg Concertos, written during his years at Cöthen (1717 - 1723), were influenced by Italian Composers (including Vivaldi).

These reflect the Baroque Era, a creative period of new exploration of ideas and innovation in the arts.

Architecture was ornate and highly decorative. Gilded paintings (covered in gold) and wall paintings (frescoes) adorned the interior walls and ceilings.

This decorative element in art was translated into decorative ornamentation in music.

In 1719 Bach performed for Christian Ludwig, Margrave (a type of nobleman) of Brandenburg. He was so impressed with Bach's music that he commissioned (asked for) him to submit some pieces for his orchestra.

Two years later, in 1721, Bach's six Brandenburg Concertos were dedicated to Christian Ludwig, Margrave of Brandenburg, as Bach hoped to secure more work from the Margrave. The Margrave however, sent the works to the library and did not acknowledge receipt of the works, never heard them and never paid Bach!

Perhaps because they were delivered two years late or because the Orchestra of Margrave had only 6 players, this large scale instrumental work was not performed at that time. Luckily, we do get to hear them!

Go to **GSGMUSIC.com** - For Easy Access to listening to Bach's Brandenburg Concerto No. 5 BWV 1050. Performing Forces: *concertino* (flute, violin and harpsichord) and *ripieno* (string orchestra). Enjoy watching.

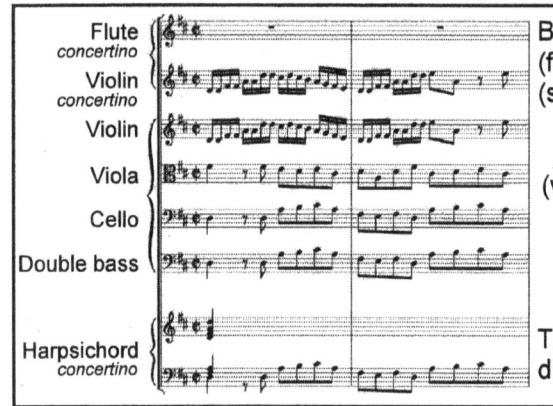

Bach's Concerto grosso (*concerti grossi*) is in 3 movements (fast, slow, fast). It is performed by the Baroque Orchestra (small ensemble), 2 contrasting groups of Performing Forces:

Group #1: *ripieno (or "tutti")* - string orchestra (violins, violas, cellos & double basses play "tutti", all together)

Group #2: *concertino* - a group of solo instruments (First Mvt: flute, violin and harpsichord)

The role of "conductor" was often the harpsichordist who directed the Baroque Orchestra ensemble from the keyboard.

1. The Brandenburg Concertos are in the Genre of *concerto grosso* and were composed by __Bach__.

2. The *concerti grossi* is usually in three movements with tempos of __fast__, __slow__, __fast__.

3. The *concerti grossi* string orchestra (violins, violas, cellos & double basses) is called __ripieno (tutti)__.

4. The *concerti grossi* group of solo instruments (flute, violin & harpsichord) is called __concertino__.

5. Concerto grosso (*concerti grossi*) means __more than one soloist and orchestra__.

MUSIC HISTORY - J.S. BACH - BRANDENBURG CONCERTO NO. 5 FIRST MOVEMENT BWV 1050

Bach's Brandenburg Concertos (set of six concertos) are in 3 movements. Each concerto grosso features two contrasting groups of different instruments, played both separately and in combination with each other. This creates tonal contrast between the lighter texture of *concertino* and denser texture of the *ripieno (tutti)*.

Brandenburg Concerto No. 5 in D Major First Movement, tempo - *allegro*, is in *ritornello* form (often used in the first and third movements of a concerto grosso).

Ritornello* Form** is based on the shifts between the ***ripieno (or ***tutti***, the accompanying group of string instruments) who open the piece with the ***ritornello*** (the main theme or refrain repeated throughout the movement), and the ***concertino*** (the solo group of instruments that included the violin, flute and harpsichord) who play *episodes* (contrasting sections played by the soloists).

1. Analyze the *ritornello* (main theme), introduced by the violins at the beginning of the Concerto No. 5 First Movement, by answering the questions below. (All other instruments play as accompaniment, *ripieno*).

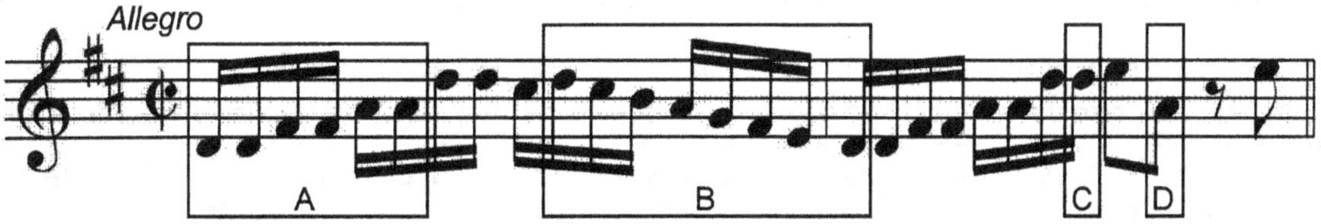

a) Name the key. __D Major__ Identify the Time Signature. __cut time (2/2 time)__

b) Name and explain the tempo of this piece. __Allegro - fast__

c) At letter A, identify the triad. Root: __D__ Type/Quality: __Major__ Position: __root pos__

d) At letter B, name the descending scale: __D Major scale__ Name the Tonic note: __D__

e) Name the type of notes (note values) used for the driving rhythm in measure 1: __sixteenth notes__

f) At letter C, name the note: __D__ Give the Technical Degree Name: __Tonic__

g) At letter D, name the note: __A__ Give the Technical Degree Name: __Dominant__

2. Listen to Brandenburg Concerto No. 5 First Movement. Check (✓) the correct answer below.

The Performing Forces of Brandenburg Concerto No. 5 First Movement are:	
✓ *concertino* (violin, flute, harpsichord) & *ripieno*	☐ SATB Chorus & Orchestra

The composer of the Brandenburg Concerto No. 5 First Movement is:	
✓ J. S. Bach	☐ A. L. Vivaldi

The Genre of Brandenburg Concerto No. 5 First Movement is:	
☐ oratorio	✓ concerto grosso

MUSIC HISTORY - J.S. BACH - BRANDENBURG CONCERTO NO. 5 FIRST MVT - RITORNELLO FORM

Brandenburg Concerto No. 5 in D Major First Movement, *Ritornello* form alternates between the *ripieno (tutti)* and the *concertino* sections, featuring three solo instruments: Violin, Flute and Harpsichord.

Ritornello Form - structuring device for the First Movement. Ritornello opens and closes the movement in the Tonic, and appears at points in between **"Episodes"** to stabilize the various keys to which the music modulates. Each Episode is performed by a different solo member of the Concertino.

| *Ritornello* Ripieno (refrain) Tutti Original Key | *Episode* Concertino Flute | *Ritornello* Ripieno (refrain) Tutti | *Episode* Concertino Violin | *Ritornello* Ripieno (refrain) Tutti | *Episode* Concertino Harpsichord | *Ritornello* Ripieno (refrain) Tutti Original Key |

← Various Keys →

Concertino - The Flute solo saw immense historical significance as Bach's Brandenburg Concerto was the first composition to use the flute in a concerto setting. This influenced composers such as Vivaldi and C.P.E. Bach to compose concerti for flute as well. (*Flauto traverso* - held laterally.)

A Baroque Flute was made of wood, had finger holes and only one metal key.

Concertino - The Violin solo required incredible skill to bring out the innate qualities, a wide range of depth in emotion and mellow sounds. The bow, made from gut string (sheep intestines), was about 3/4 the length of a modern bow, which makes it easier to bounce around playfully.

A Baroque Violin had no chin rest and did not facilitate a loud sound due to the fingerboard angle.

Go to **GSGMUSIC.com** - For Easy Access to listening to Bach's Brandenburg Concerto No. 5 BWV 1050. See the full score as you listen to contrasting sounds and explore the music in Ritornello Form.

1. Analyze the imitative dialogue between the flute and the violin by answering the questions below.

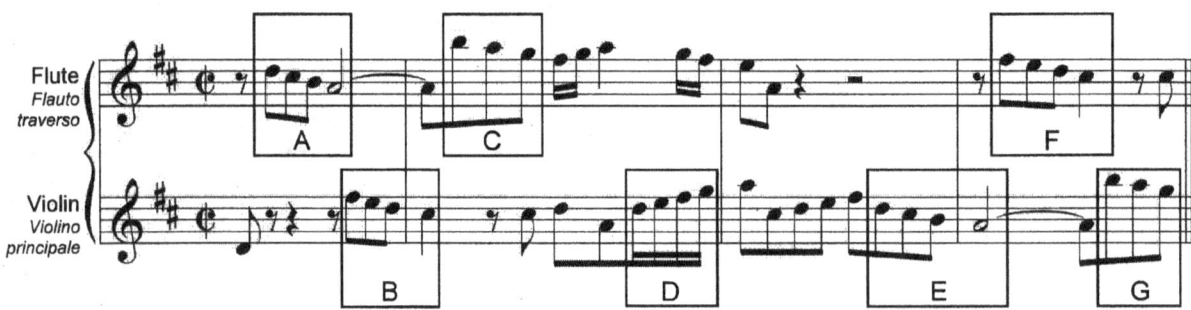

a) Circle if the melodic pattern at letter A (flute) and letter B (violin) is: (same) similar or different.

b) Circle if the rhythmic pattern at letter A and letter B is: same, (similar) or different.

c) Circle if the melodic pattern at letter C and letter D is: same, similar or (different).

d) Circle if the pattern at letter E, imitated at letter F is: rhythmic imitation or (melodic imitation).

e) Circle if the notes played at letter C, imitated at letter G are the: (same pitch) or different pitch.

f) Circle if the instruments played at letter C and letter G sound at the: same timbre or (different timbre).

MUSIC HISTORY - J.S. BACH - BRANDENBURG CONCERTO NO. 5 FIRST MVT - CONCERTINO

The *concertino* climax of the Brandenburg Concerto is one of the greatest virtuoso keyboard passages of all time. The harpsichordist, initially just an accompanist, pushes to the front to become the Ultimate Virtuoso, performing a written-out (not improvised) cadenza in a spectacular display of virtuosity.

Concertino - The Harpsichord (or *Cembalo*) solo required expert musicianship skills to master the technical challenges of the finger dexterity in its rapid rhythmic and melodic configurations. The *cadenza* (virtuoso solo passage) concludes the magnificent work.

A Baroque Harpsichord is played by striking a key, which controls the plucking of the string. There is no dynamic variation on any one key. Playing terraced dynamics (fp) requires a double manual keyboard harpsichord, which controls another set of strings.

Go to **GSGMUSIC.com** - For Easy Access to listening to Bach's Brandenburg Concerto No. 5 BWV 1050. Watch the virtuoso performance of the harpsichordist. Imagine how many hours the performer practiced!

1. Analyze the excerpt of the concertino for harpsichord (*cembalo*) by answering the questions below.

   a) At letter A, identify the triad. Root: **A**   Type/Quality: **Major**   Position: **2nd inv**

   b) The ornamentation used to decorate the music in measure 2 is called a **mordent**.

   c) Circle if the rhythmic pattern in the Bass staff in m. 1 and m. 2 is the: same, (similar) or different.

   d) Circle if the rhythmic pattern in the Bass staff in m. 1 and m. 3 is the: same, similar or (different).

   e) Circle if the concertino rapid finger dexterity is needed in the: right hand, left hand or (both hands).

2. Listen to Brandenburg Concerto No. 5 First Movement. Check (✓) the correct answer below.

The most virtuoso instrument in the three concertinos from Brandenburg Concerto No. 5 First Mvt. is the:
☐ violin ☐ flute ☑ harpsichord

The virtuoso solo passage written-out (not improvised) is called a:
☐ *concertino* ☑ *cadenza* ☐ *cembalo*

The Brandenburg Concerto No. 5 uses a structuring device for the First Movement called:
☑ ritornello form ☐ ternary form ☐ sonata form

MUSIC HISTORY - CLASSICAL ERA (1750 - 1825) and MOZART

Three masters of the **Classical Era** are Haydn, Mozart and Beethoven, one of the most beloved being Wolfgang Amadeus Mozart (1756 - 1791). Mozart's relationship with "his idol" the older Haydn, known as "the Father of the String Quartet" and the sonata-allegro form, influenced Mozart's structuring of his works.

Mozart, a "musical genius", explored the Major-minor system, homophonic texture and the sonata form. He wrote in many different genres, as you learned in the UMT Supplemental Workbooks LEVEL 2 and LEVEL 5.

UMT Level	Genre	Wolfgang Amadeus Mozart (1756 - 1791) Works
LEVEL 2	Theme & Variations	Twelve Variations on Ah vous dirai-je, Maman K 265
	Concerto	Horn Concerto No. 4 in E flat Major K 495
LEVEL 5	Opera	The Magic Flute K 620 - Queen of the Night Aria
LEVEL 6	Chamber Music	Eine kleine Nachtmusik K 525 First Movement

Mozart's Eine kleine Nachtmusik (German: "A Little Serenade" - "A Little Night Music"), Serenade No. 13 for strings in G Major K 525, was written for entertainment in 1787.

Eine kleine Nachtmusik is a chamber ensemble, courtship serenade (*serenata*), light music for violin, viola, cello and *optional double bass, with lively and memorable melodies.

"The music is not in the notes, but in the silence between."
~ Wolfgang Amadeus Mozart

Go to **GSGMUSIC.com** - For Easy Access to listening to Mozart's Eine kleine Nachtmusik First Movement. Performing Forces: string chamber orchestra (violins, violas, cellos and *double bass). Enjoy watching.

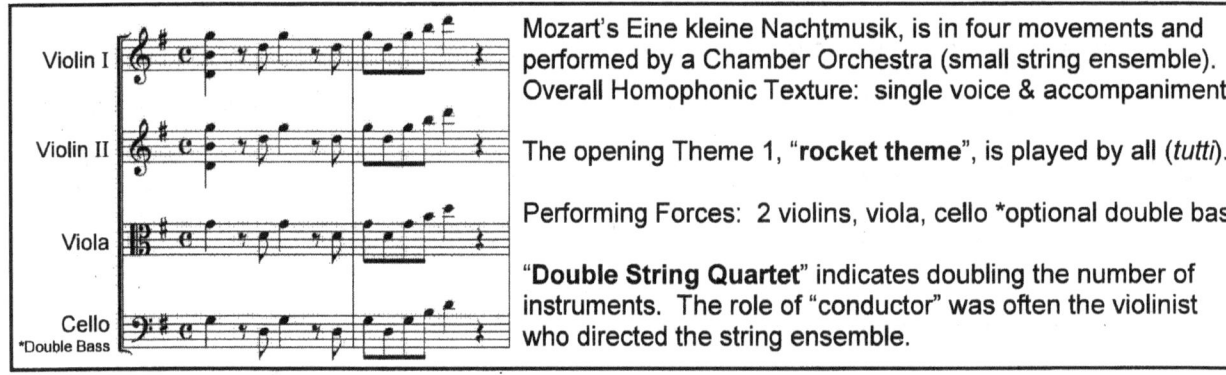

Mozart's Eine kleine Nachtmusik, is in four movements and performed by a Chamber Orchestra (small string ensemble). Overall Homophonic Texture: single voice & accompaniment.

The opening Theme 1, "**rocket theme**", is played by all (*tutti*).

Performing Forces: 2 violins, viola, cello *optional double bass.

"**Double String Quartet**" indicates doubling the number of instruments. The role of "conductor" was often the violinist who directed the string ensemble.

1. Name the Era or Period of W. A. Mozart as: Baroque, Classical or Romantic. _Classical_
2. Eine kleine Nachtmusik (German), in English means _A little Serenade/A little Night Music_
3. The opening Theme 1 "rocket theme" in Eine kleine Nachtmusik is played by _All (tutti)_.
4. Mozart's Eine kleine Nachtmusik, *Allegro*, was written in 1787 for _entertainment_.
5. Mozart used a melodic line single voice and accompaniment called _homophonic_ texture.
6. The Genre of Mozart's Eine kleine Nachtmusik is called _Chamber Music_.
7. Eine kleine Nachtmusik was written for Performing Forces: _2 violins, viola, cello (double bass)_

MUSIC HISTORY - W.A. MOZART - EINE KLEINE NACHTMUSIK - EXPOSITION - THEME 1, 2a & 2b

Mozart's Eine kleine Nachtmusik in G Major First Movement is in Sonata-Allegro Form, one of the most important forms developed in the Classical Era (starting with Haydn, then Mozart and later, Beethoven). Sonata-Allegro Form is an expansion of the Rounded Binary Form ||:A :||:B A1 :|| into 3 sections: Exposition (A), Development (B), Recapitulation (A1). The second half, B A1, is not repeated in sonata form.

Exposition - statement that contains two contrasting themes. Theme 1 in the Tonic key of G Major is a disjunct marchlike "rocket" theme that ascends quickly with symmetrical phrasing and ends with an Authentic Cadence in G Major. A bridge modulates to Theme 2a and Theme 2b in the Dominant key of D Major, a conjunct graceful theme that feels less hurried.

1. Analyze the Exposition excerpt Theme 1 in G Major by answering the questions below.

Theme 1 - "Rocket Theme Motive"

a) The 9 note musical pattern in mm. 1 - 2 of the marchlike Theme 1 is called the __Rocket__ theme.

b) At letter A, name: Root/Quality Chord Symbol: __G/D__ Type/Quality: __Major__ Scale Degree: __Tonic__

c) At letter B, name: Root/Quality Chord Symbol: __D⁷__ Type/Quality: __Dom 7__ Scale Degree: __Dominant__

2. Analyze the Exposition excerpts Theme 2a and 2b Motives in D Major by answering the questions below.

Theme 2a Motive   Motive

a) Theme 1 notes move by leap, contrasting with Theme 2a as the first 5 notes move by __step__.

b) "Rocket Theme" 1 is ascending, contrasting with Theme 2a as the first 5 notes are __descending__.

c) Theme 1 quarter & eighth notes contrast with Theme 2a, a new rhythm of triplet __sixteenth__ notes.

Theme 2b Motive   Motive

d) Theme 1 dynamics are __f__, contrasting with Theme 2a and 2b where the dynamics are __p__.

e) Theme 1 is in the key of __G__ Major, contrasting with Theme 2a and 2b in the key of __D__ Major.

f) The insistent repeated seven note rhythmic motive in Theme 2b are all __eighth__ notes.

MUSIC HISTORY - W.A. MOZART- EINE KLEINE NACHTMUSIK - DEVELOPMENT & RECAPITULATION

Mozart's Eine kleine Nachtmusik in G Major First Movement, Sonata-Allegro Form is in three sections: Exposition (mm. 1 - 55), Development (mm. 56 - 75), and Recapitulation (mm. 76 - 137).

> The term "First Movement Form" (Sonata-Allegro Form) is applied to Sonata Form because it is often the first movement in a multi-movement work such as Eine kleine Nachtmusik. The term *sonata* refers to both the sonata form and to the multi-movement structure found in sonatas, string quartets, symphonies, etc.

Development: Departure from the Tonic key presenting new musical ideas developed from the theme(s). Theme 1 is presented in D Major in this short development section. It quickly moves to C Major using ideas from Theme 2b. This section ends on the Dominant, returning to the Tonic key in the Recapitulation.

1. Analyze the Development section excerpt by answering the questions below.

Theme 1 "Rocket Theme" Motive

a) Exposition Theme 1 in G Major is transposed in the Development section into the key of **D Major**.

b) At letter A, name: Root/Quality Chord Symbol: **D/A** Type/Quality: **Major** Position: **2nd inv**

c) At letter B, name: Root/Quality Chord Symbol: **B** Type/Quality: **Major** Position: **Root pos**

Recapitulation: Restatement of the entire Exposition but with all sections now in the Tonic key. The bridge changes slightly because it doesn't modulate. Coda, an optional feature in Sonata Form, ends the movement with six measures of strong repeated Authentic Cadence chords to conclude the First Movement.

2. Analyze the Recapitulation section excerpt by answering the questions below.

Theme 2a Motive   Motive

a) Exposition Theme 2a in D Major is transposed in the Recapitulation section into the key of **G Major**.

b) At letter A, name: Root/Quality Chord Symbol: **Am** Type/Quality: **minor** Scale Degree: **Supertonic**

c) Circle if the repeated Theme 2a Motive is: inversion   or   augmentation   or   (**transposition**)

Go to **GSGMUSIC.com** - For Easy Access to listening to Mozart's Eine kleine Nachtmusik, all 4 Movements. Performances will vary from string ensemble to vocal ensemble to "Fun at the Office". Enjoy watching.

MUSIC HISTORY - BAROQUE & CLASSICAL - REVIEW CHART

In the UMT Supplemental Series you have learned about Music Time Periods (Eras), Instruments, Voices, Genres, Form, Composers and their Works, and how to analyze music by listening and looking at the score.

Go to GSGMUSIC.com - For Easy Access to Watching Videos and Listening to Various Genres of Music. Identify the Performing Forces, Form, Character, Mood & Relationship to Text. Analyze the Rhythm, Meter, Melody, Harmony, Dynamics, Timbre, Texture, Vocal Ranges and Instruments that create each unique work.

1. Complete the Music History Baroque & Classical Review Chart below.

Invention in C Major No. 1 BWV 772 Composer: **Bach** Period: **Baroque**

Genre: **Solo Keyboard** Texture: **polyphonic with imitative counterpoint**

Compositional Devices: **imitation, inversion, augmentation, sequence**

Performing Forces: **harpsichord or clavichord (and now piano)**

Eine kleine Nachtmusik, K 525, First Mvt. Composer: **Mozart** Period: **Classical**

Genre: **Chamber Music** Form: **Sonata-Allegro Form**

Name 3 Sections of the Form: **Exposition**, **Development**, **Recapitulation**

Performing Forces: **2 violins, viola, cello (double bass) or small string orchestra**

Hallelujah Chorus from Messiah Composer: **Handel** Period: **Baroque** Genre: **Oratorio**

When music reflects the literal meaning of the text, the technique is: **word painting**

Describe one way the music expresses the word "Hallelujah": **Harmony for Hallelujah IV-I many Amen's + Plagal progressions**

Performing Forces: **SATB chorus and orchestra**

Queen of the Night - The Magic Flute Composer: **Mozart** Period: **Classical**

Genre: **Opera** Queen of the Night Aria - the Queen expresses desire for: **revenge**

Define: aria **Solo song expressing feelings** libretto **text of the story**

Performing Forces: **Coloratura Soprano and Orchestra**

Brandenburg Concerto No. 5 First Mvt. BWV 1050 Composer: **Bach** Period: **Baroque**

Genre: **Concerto** Form: **Ritornello Form**

Define: concertino **group of solo instruments** ripieno **full string orchestra**

Performing Forces: **Concertino - harpsichord, violin, flute + ripieno (string orchestra)**

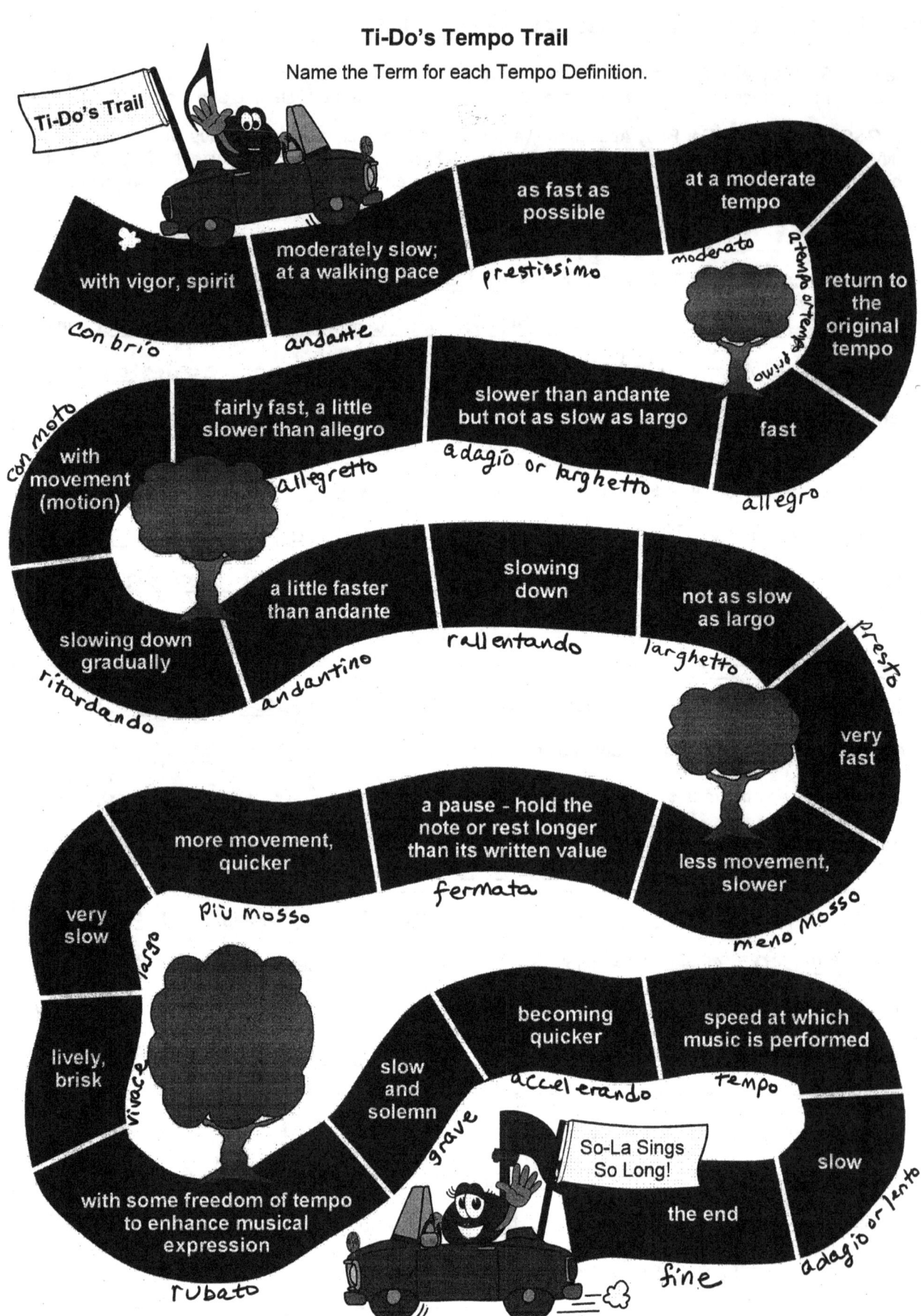

Ultimate Music Theory
Level 6 Theory Exam

Total Score: ___ / 100

The Ultimate Music Theory™ Rudiments Workbooks, Supplemental Workbooks and Exams prepare students for successful completion of the Royal Conservatory of Music Theory Levels.

1. a) Name the following intervals.

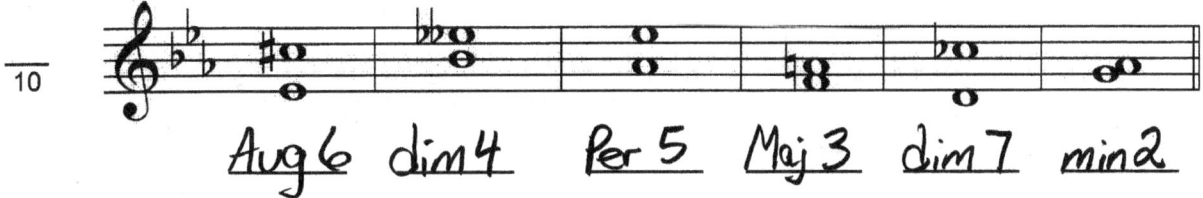

Aug 6   dim 4   Per 5   Maj 3   dim 7   min 2

b) Change the upper (top) note of each of the above intervals enharmonically (either making the interval larger OR making the interval smaller). Rename each chromatically altered interval.

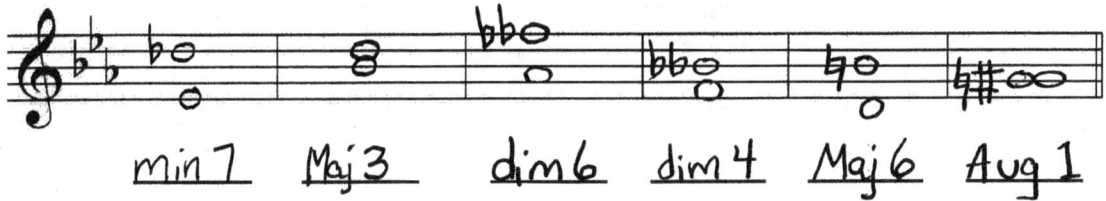

min 7   Maj 3   dim 6   dim 4   Maj 6   Aug 1

2. a) Rewrite each broken chord in solid/blocked form directly below each measure. Use half notes. Write the Root/Quality Chord Symbol above and the Functional Chord Symbol below each solid chord.

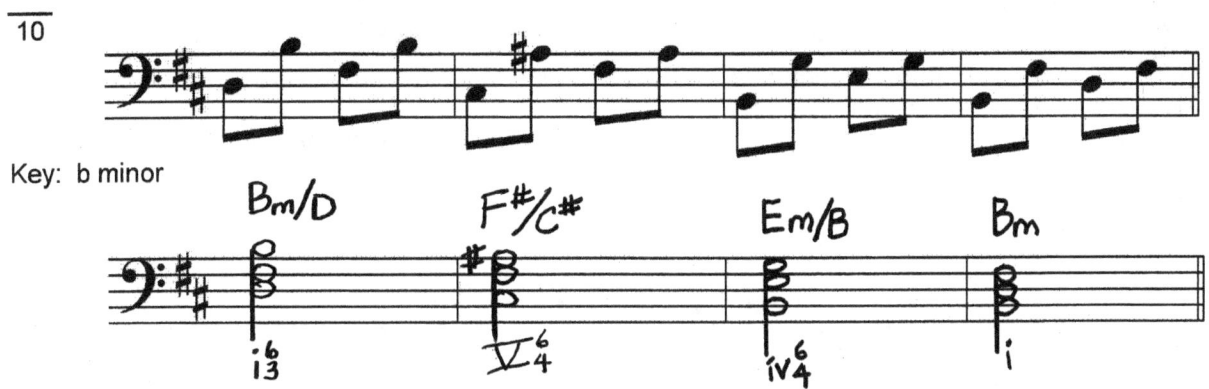

Key: b minor

b) Write the following chords in solid/blocked form for each of the given Functional Chord Symbols. Use whole notes.

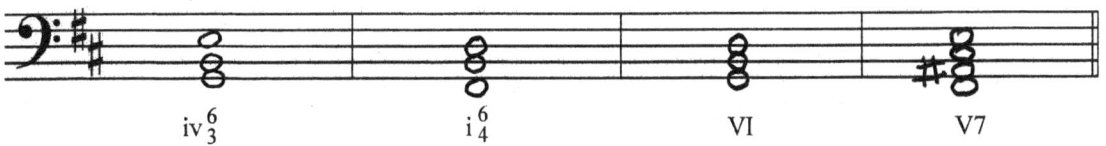

iv_3^6 i_4^6 VI   V7

UltimateMusicTheory.com © Copyright 2017 Gloryland Publishing. All Rights Reserved.

Ultimate Music Theory
Level 6 Theory Exam

3. a) Add bar lines to complete each rhythm.

b) Add the rest(s) below each bracket to complete each measure.

4. This Musical Excerpt is from J.P. Kirnberger's "Les carillons".
   a) Name the key of the excerpt.
   b) Arrange the notes in each box into a closed root position triad or chord on the staff provided.
   c) Name the Root, the Quality and the Position of each triad or chord.

Excerpt Key: a minor

A:
Root: A
Quality: minor
Position: root pos

B:
Root: E
Quality: Dom 7th
Position: root pos

Ultimate Music Theory
Level 6 Theory Exam

5. a) For each of the following phrases:
   i) Name the key.
   ii) Write the correct Time Signature below the bracket.

Key: e♭ minor

Key: E Major

Key: g minor

b) For each of the following phrases:
   i) Name the key.
   ii) Write the Root/Quality Chord Symbol above each chord in the Cadence on the lines provided.
   iii) Write the Functional Chord Symbol below each chord in the Cadence on the lines provided.
   iv) Name the type of Cadence as Authentic (Perfect) or Half (Imperfect).

Key: F♯ Major   Key: b♭ minor
Cadence: Half Cadence   Cadence: Authentic Cadence

Ultimate Music Theory
Level 6 Theory Exam

6. Write the following scales, ascending and descending. Use a Key Signature and any necessary accidentals. Use whole notes.

10 a) The relative minor scale, harmonic form, of A Major in the Treble Clef. (f# minor harmonic)

b) The Tonic Major scale (Parallel Major) of d minor in the Bass Clef. (D Major)

c) a sharp minor melodic scale in the Bass Clef. (a# minor melodic)

d) The relative Major scale of b flat minor in the Treble Clef. (Db Major)

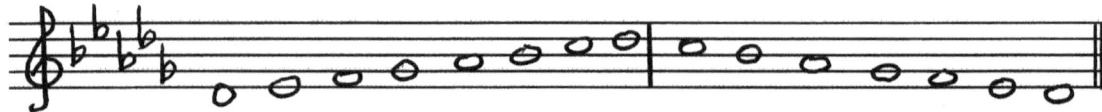

e) The Tonic minor scale (Parallel minor) natural form of C Major in the Treble Clef. (C minor natural)

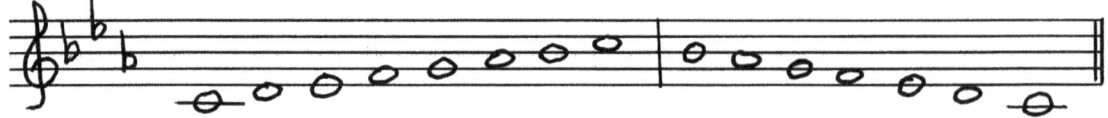

f) Fill in the blanks to identify each of the following note names.

The Leading Tone of c sharp minor melodic scale: __B#__.

The Subtonic of a flat minor natural scale: __Gb__.

The Leading Tone of G flat Major scale: __F__.

The Subdominant of f sharp minor harmonic scale: __B__.

The Dominant of D flat Major scale: __Ab__.

Ultimate Music Theory
Level 6 Theory Exam

7. a) Name the key of this melody. Write the Time Signature on the music below the bracket.
    b) Complete the first phrase ending on an unstable scale degree. Label the degree above the note.
    c) Compose a four-measure Answer phrase to create a Parallel Period ending on a stable scale degree. Label the degree above the note.
    d) Draw a phrase mark over each phrase. (one possible answer)

___
10

Key: F Major

e) Transpose the melody up an augmented fourth into the Treble Clef. Use the correct Key Signature and name the new Key.

Key: C Major

Key: F# Major

f) Transpose the given melody up into the key of D flat Major. Use the correct Key Signature. Name the interval of transposition between the given key and the new key.

Key: C Major transposed up to D flat Major. The interval of transposition is a minor 2.

Ultimate Music Theory
Level 6 Theory Exam

8. Answer the following Music History questions by filling in the blanks.

__10__

a) Name the Composer of Invention in C Major, BWV 772. __J.S. Bach__

b) Name the predominant texture of Invention in C Major, BWV 772. __polyphonic__

c) Name the Composer of Brandenburg Concerto No. 5. __J.S. Bach__

d) Name the Genre of Brandenburg Concerto No. 5. __Concerto grosso__

e) Name 1 solo instrument featured in Brandenburg Concerto No. 5. __Violin (flute, harpsichord)__

f) Identify the form used to open and close Mvmt. 1 of the Concerto No. 5. __ritornello__

g) Name the Composer of Eine kleine Nachtmusik. __W. A. Mozart__

h) Name the Genre of Eine kleine Nachtmusick. __Chamber Music__

i) Name the form of the 1st Movement of Eine kleine Nachtmusik. __Sonata (sonata-allegro)__

j) Identify the name given to the disjunct opening Theme 1 in Eine kleine Nachtmusik. __Rocket theme__

9. Match each musical term or sign with the English definition. (Not all definitions will be used.)

__10__

Term		Definition
tranquillo ed piano	c	a) very, very slow and graceful
più spiritoso	e	b) slow, but not too much
subito andantino	j	c) quiet, tranquil and soft
quasi rubato	l	d) at the liberty of the performer
molto largo e grazia	a	e) more spirited
sempre leggiero	f	f) always light, nimble, quick
lento ma non troppo	b	g) loud, then suddenly soft and with movement, motion
fortepiano ed con moto	g	h) little by little becoming softer
senza una corda	k	i) (much), very fast
molto allegro	i	j) suddenly, a little faster than andante
poco a poco diminuendo	h	k) without the left pedal (soft pedal on the piano)
		l) as if with some freedom of tempo to enhance musical expression

Ultimate Music Theory
Level 6 Theory Exam

10. Analyze Mozart's Menuetto I by answering the questions below.

a) Add the correct Time Signature. Circle if this is in: (Simple Time) or Compound Time.
b) Circle if this Menuetto I was written during the: Baroque Period or (Classical Period)
c) Label the two sections in this piece as A and B. Name the form of this piece. __Binary Form__
d) Circle if the texture of this piece is: monophonic or (homophonic) or polyphonic
e) Name the interval at the letters A: __Per 4__ B: __Maj 3__ C: __min 2__
f) Identify the Cadence implied by the Bass Notes at the letter D as: (Authentic) or Half.
g) For the triad at the letter E, identify the: Root: __F__ Type: __Major__ Position: __root pos__
h) Identify the Cadence implied by the Bass Notes at the letter F as: (Authentic) or Half.
i) Circle a Chromatic Half Step directly on the music. Label it CH. Name the interval. __Aug 1__
j) Circle a Diatonic Half Step directly on the music. Label it DH. Name the interval. __min 2__

Ultimate Music Theory Certificate

_____

has successfully completed all the requirements of the

Music Theory Level 6

_____   _____
Music Teacher   *Date*

Enriching Lives Through Music Education

www.ingramcontent.com/pod-product-compliance
Lightning Source LLC
Chambersburg PA
CBHW081730100526
44591CB00016B/2562